PATHWAYS
to *Her Rise*

**PERSONAL STORIES AND PRACTICAL
ADVICE FROM COURAGEOUS
WOMEN ON THE RISE**

PRESENTED BY
Marsha Guerrier

Printed and bound in the United States of America

First Printing March 2021

ISBN 978-0-9991297-8-4

Library of Congress Control Number: 2021901815

Published by: Women on the Rise NY

Table of Content

"

I had to make my own living and my own opportunity. But I made it! Don't sit down and wait for the opportunities to come. Get up and make them.

- Madam C.J. Walker

"

Becoming Her

by Marsha Guerrier

Women of color in many industries have shared experiences of helping corporations advance and grow while they are left undervalued and underestimated. Though many women of color are leaving Corporate America for entrepreneurship, for many women, leaving their full-time job is not an option, they are managing both. Externally, we are dealing with unconscious bias and micro-aggressions that prohibit us from being considered for advanced positions and funding for our projects. Internally, we are dealing with imposter syndrome that holds us back from affirming our value and finding our voice as leaders.

We know that women and men are often provided different opportunities to advance in leadership roles in the workforce and because of this many women are often discouraged from entering the world of entrepreneurship. The limiting beliefs of others, imposter syndrome, fear of rejection, and the need to be perfect are the most widespread feelings that women report as to why they are either slow to start their side business or have not yet leaped to becoming their own boss. In Pathways to HerRise nine courageous women share their stories and advice on how they have been able to chart their path to success.

Before they become founders many entrepreneurs develop their skills and insight to start their business by working a full-time job, thus creating her pathway towards leadership roles. My co-authors are no different, sharing insights on how they navigated their past experiences while building a business. They have experienced challenges and barriers that may have slowed them down but never deterred them from pursuing their dreams of validation, independence, and financial freedom through entrepreneurship. Some of these barriers are both structural and mindset in nature. My journey began as a young teenager learning about business and having the good fortune to be surrounded by mentors that believed in me. Only to be faced with the limiting beliefs of others later in my career.

Despite the many mentors that I had earlier on in my life, as I navigated from student to employee I was met by several people that did not believe a young black woman can successfully lead teams that were predominately white males. Throughout my career in a male-dominated industry, I continued to demand my place in leadership even when I knew there was no chance of actually getting the role. While building resilience, I took advantage of opportunities to learn all that I could and develop my skills. I knew that no matter what, skills are transferable. Whether you decide to use those skills to find a new employer or use those skills to go off on your own, the one thing people cannot take away from you is your knowledge!

In over 25 years working in corporate environments, I have been referred to as a disrupter. My first experience in the workforce in my formative years was as a file clerk for a government agency, which helped me land my big break after leaving college on Wall Street. I worked on a trading desk for a money management firm. I manually typed all of the trades for the day into the system of our broker-dealer. Then the next morning I had to enter those same trades into a spreadsheet for the company's records. This was long before we hired a financial accounting software company (that would later be my employer) to integrate the transactions between both companies. Not long after I started to work on the trading desk, I begin to implement improvements to the way we logged the trades.

In addition to my job on the trading desk, I was asked to work on a special project to convert our firm's data into the new financial software. My ability to understand the software and the needs of a trading system advanced my role at the company. My career as an analyst took shape at this point. I became a subject matter expert in financial accounting systems and later was recruited to join that same software company. I was great at connecting with others personally and professionally. I did not know then that what I was doing was mastering the art of networking. Throughout my career, I have been referred for positions to help companies develop software because of my ability to get the job done yet, while on the job, the same barriers that most black women experienced, so have I, not being promoted and not get a raise while on the job.

Surviving several ups and downs of the financial industry, I am proud to say I have never been fired or laid off. Even though I was an integral part of several teams, I have often had to, as I call it, audition for the leadership roles that I was already doing. After being overlooked for promotion after promotion, only to be the go-to or lead person on the team, I finally needed to use my leadership skills in a way that would satisfy me and earn me extra income.

With my skills and passions, I started side businesses like events planning, catering services, home décor, and design and career coaching until I finally found the business that I was meant to do, coaching women seeking to advance in leadership. Working for several large companies as a subject matter expert, I finally decided to use my skills to help other women of color build their million-dollar brands. I work with women across all industries, lending my expertise in systems, branding, and marketing. Through HerSuiteSpot I finally feel validated for the work that I am doing from my clients who appreciate my services and level of expertise. At work, many black women are undervalued, underutilized, and underestimated. We turn to entrepreneurship as a way to fill our wage and promotion gap.

If you are searching for a pathway to rise and become a leader in your profession, I want to offer you three mindset shifts you need to be fearless in your pursuit towards leadership whether at work or in business:

The first thing is to start asking for more than your worth. The best advice I got from a mentor was to ask for more than what I wanted when searching for a new job. Especially since companies tend to give women of color fewer pay increases while they are on the job, I knew I had to come in at a higher rate from the beginning. I remember transitioning from one company to another. I asked for 50% more than what I was making. Every several years I had to change companies to give myself a raise. If you research the salary range for the position and believe that you are qualified for the job, you will succeed. You see, asking your worth is more about understanding what is amazingly unique about you. Remind yourself of what skills and values you bring to the table in time you will be able to confidently ask for your worth, whether in your career or side hustle.

Second, surround yourself with a community of people that share your values and believe in you. Like I mentioned before, almost every job opportunity presented to me was due to a connection I had to someone at the firm that would validate my skills. The same is true for my side business; some of my clients come from referrals and others from people getting to know me. The impact you make on people is a reason most successful people do well in their career or business. That old saying, "it's not what you know; it's who you know, is so true. Except it is up to you to show them what you know to maintain good relationships. Leveraging the right relationships to advance your career, will truly have a positive impact on the person that you become. Networking and relationship building is a two-way street, be prepared to give as much as you intend to receive.

Lastly, know that your past does not define your future - If I think back to when an old boss told me that I was not qualified to lead a team, I would never have had the audacity to start my own side business employing others in the process while working my 9 to 5. You see, at every stage of my personal growth, I left behind all the limitations that someone else placed on me because I knew that was greatness within me.

I am excited to present to you, Pathways to HerRise, an inspiring resource that will motivate you to discover the pathway to rise in your career and business.

About Marsha Guerrier

MARSHA GUERRIER is a TEDx Speaker, 3x Bestselling Author, Trainer, Business Analyst and Coach, and CEO of Women on the Rise NY, Inc. dba HerSuiteSpot®, a SBE and WMBE Certified private network for women of color providing leadership and entrepreneurship development. Marsha has held a career in the FinServ and FinTech industries spanning over 20 years working for Fortune 500 and startup firms, working in areas of Systems Test Engineer, Business Analysis and Product Management. Marsha is also the founder and Executive Director of the Yva Jourdan Foundation a non-profit organization dedicated to strengthen the leadership, power, and voices of women and children through our educational programs.

Marsha holds a Bachelors of Science in Business, Management and Economics. She is a two time recipient of the State Assembly of New York's Women of Distinction Award for her work with the Yva Jourdan Foundation and Women on the Rise NY, Inc. Marsha is a member of the Nassau County Comptroller MWBE Steering Committee, the Female & Finances, Female Founders Collective and the Forbes Women's Forum. Marsha has been featured on Open on Bronxnet, Radio 103.9 NY, Next Nation Sirius XM, 90.3 WHPC, Newsday, Patch and other media outlets. I have had the pleasure to working with Amazon, Unilever, Forbes, Bloomberg, BackStage Capital, Microsoft, Oprah Magazine, National Grid, New York Community Bank, NBA, National Coalition of 100 Black Women, Dress For Success, Finastra and many other organizations.

Find Marsha online at:

www.hersuitespot.com

"

The only way you really see change,
is by helping create it.

– Lena Waithe

"

Grow, Encourage, Empower

by Gretchen Campbell

I'm a Licensed Clinical Mental Health Clinician, Psychotherapist, and owner of a group practice in Raleigh/Durham North Carolina with over 19 years of experience in the mental health field. I started my career in New Jersey and gained a lot of experience working in various environments across different races and ethnicities. I knew very early on that I wanted to go into private practice but didn't have a clear plan of how this might come to fruition. When I relocated to North Carolina in 2009, navigating the workforce was challenging because the mental health system was also different.

In 2015, after changing employers a total of four times for various reasons, I knew it was time for me to start the entrepreneurial journey that would allow me to serve my community on my own terms. That is when I gave birth to Grow, Encourage, Empower PLLC, a private practice serving the child and adolescent population. Taking that first step was very scary. That is why I started on a part-time basis, while still working my full-time job. This allowed me to establish roots in my business, build a name for myself within the community, and prepare myself for the highs and lows of entrepreneurship. It also pushed me to work harder, servicing the child/adolescent population managing symptoms of depression, anxiety, and other mental health and behavioral issues. I also started to build a niche for working with mothers and daughters, a population I had been passionate about but seldom had the opportunity to serve.

Starting my business on a part-time basis provided me with the time I needed to think about transitioning the business from part-time to full-time, while still earning a full-time salary. It gave me the opportunity to create a growth plan and save, so financially I would feel secure once I finally decided to make the full-time leap. I'll be honest; I did not have a definitive date for when that leap might be. However, in 2017, two years after I started the business, I quit my full-time job. It didn't go quite as I had planned; but because of circumstances with my last employer, I knew that it was time for me to take the leap. Financially, I'd been saving for a few months and my business was making enough on a part-time basis. I knew it would be able to sustain me and the lifestyle I created for myself if I was 100% focused on growing it. This was definitely a scary time but something that I was committed to and willing to put in the work. I knew the fear was the only thing holding me back at this point, and I needed to shift my focus and make growing my business a priority.

Over the years, I have learned that the entrepreneurial journey is different for everyone and there are different seasons for each stage of the business. One thing that remains the same throughout each stage for me is being committed during the ups and downs. I've experienced physical, emotional, and financial highs and lows as an entrepreneur, and I have come to the conclusion that these experiences are inevitable.

I've learned through it all, remaining positive and believing in that yourself is critical, especially on those rough days. It is also extremely important to have a support system or a cheering squad throughout the process. Having my parents during the initial transition was extremely helpful. When I first told them I was quitting my job to focus on my private practice full-time their immediate response was, "We are so proud of you". That was so encouraging. I think I needed someone else to affirm for me that it was possible, and they have been rock solid every step of the way. It's also been critical to have other therapists who are on the same journey cheer you on for each milestone. They become the cheerleaders that remind you you're doing an awesome job but also encourage you to take care of yourself.

Having a healthy balance between my work and personal life has been crucial to me remaining in business and being calculated as I grow and change the business structure. There have been moments when I wanted to add services or create something new but being mindful of burnout, I had to take into account how much I already had on my plate and what the additional workload would require. It's also helped me to put into perspective what I can source out so that I am able to grow the business. Coming to terms with my need to run all legs of the business, but still wanting time to do other things, helped me to realize that as a business owner, you must know when to ask for help or employ other sources.

When I first started it was easy for me to do everything but as the business grew I learned that continuing this pattern could possibly hurt the business because things were beginning to suffer. So, I added someone to the team to manage the finances. This provided me with peace of mind knowing all of the financial obligations were being handled. And as the business continues to grow so will the team, according to the tasks you no longer have to do on your own. Your main function becomes to manage the operational part of the business so you can concentrate more on the parts you are most passionate about.

Being in the position where I've begun to hire other clinicians has made me think back to times where I was an employee. Having the experience of working for and in multiple environments has afforded me the opportunity to see both sides. I've worked for others who were running a business that was very similar whether it was privately owned and/or for larger companies. I think having that experience helped me to see why the small nuances are important when it comes to being an employer and critical to running a successful business. It has also helped me to look at my role as an owner in a different way and to be proactive about checking in with my team weekly. It is important to make sure their needs are being met and to see if there is anything I can do to help them be successful in their role. As I write this, I am sending a text message to one of my employees, checking in on them to see what may be needed for the week ahead. I am also thinking about creating a system to ensure I am always coming from a supportive position, something I didn't always feel when I was on the other end. Taking care of those on your team is an important part of running a successful business because they are key pieces to helping you continue to grow.

I can remember when I first began my entrepreneurial journey and was still working full-time. Knowing that one day I would eventually be my own boss, I started to shift the way I thought about my position. I started to view my employers as investors because I knew I needed the money to continue living but also it was helping to fund my dream. I think this is important for any entrepreneur who is still working full-time when you want to have a smooth transition.

Leaving a job prematurely can be a setback, especially if you haven't considered what it will take physically, emotionally, and financially for you to continue living the life you've created for yourself while starting your own business. There were definitely times where I wanted to take the leap before I actually did, but I also knew financially the business was not able to sustain me as yet. This was also a motivating factor for me as I began to think about my practice. There were some critical and risky decisions that had to be made to build and grow.

When I was in year two of my business, I decided to move locations. Depending on your business, this might not seem like much, but as a therapist location means a lot. When someone is searching for a therapist, they are typically looking for someone in close proximity. My very first location was right off of a major highway in the same vicinity as other therapists. In fact, the first building I was in was with other therapists so we had the luxury to refer clients to one another and lean on each other for support if needed. So when I decided to move, I knew it was a risk because my current clients could decide it was too far from them and the potential new clients might not think my new location was convenient enough. Oddly enough, it was the best move for my business. Even though the location wasn't off of a major highway, my client caseload almost tripled immediately. Due to the new location, I changed my marketing strategy, which led to an increase in clients and a surge in a population that I was passionate about serving. The move even changed how I viewed my community because now my practice was in the town where I lived. I was able to see the lack of diversity in businesses. I started to see how I wanted to show up in my community and what gaps I might be able to fill. The new location encouraged me to imagine "What could be?" but it was also lacking the space I needed to grow and expand. So I remained at that location for almost two years before moving again.

This time the move was less scary because I knew it would allow the business to grow while serving a much-needed community. However, once again, I moved to a location that would not only allow me to have multiple offices, but I was able to offer different services that were under the business model that I dreamed of. My goal was to have space where I could offer multiple wellness services under one roof. If I hadn't taken the time to write out clear goals for the vision I had, I would not have made this strategic decision. Once I was in this new space, I was able to offer additional services, hire other clinicians, and dream of other possibilities. What I didn't expect, which I am sure most business owners didn't, was right in the midst of all of the growth we would be faced with the Covid-19 pandemic.

Providing a service that is typically and historically done face to face, managing this hurdle has been no small task. Making the difficult decision of when to end face-to-face sessions at the beginning of a pandemic, worrying about how many clients would want to wait to resume in-person sessions, and worrying how insurance providers would manage this was extremely scary and something I hadn't prepared for. What I have learned is that when you are in business being able to pivot is extremely important. Many of the goals I established for 2020 had to be put on hold. Now I had to figure out how to continue pushing the business forward to sustain. Luckily, I had not yet begun to rent out additional space at my current location even though I had already hired two clinicians to meet the needs of the clients that I projected the business to gain. It was also helpful that the clinicians were contractors and not full-time employees so they had full-time jobs and weren't dependent upon employment with Grow, Encourage, Empower to sustain them. However, I still had some tough decisions to make. I had to let my assistant go, and I was now placed back in the role of doing all of the administrative tasks again. I also closed down one of my locations as most of those clients would be returning home because they were college students at a local University and were being required to leave campus.

I then had to figure out the best plan to continue serving my clients. This is when having colleagues and/or other people who are in the same industry can be helpful. We were all in the same boat and navigating this transition together. I was now in a position where each decision I made was critical to sustaining the business. Thankfully, I had financial systems in place prior to growing the business that would help me to navigate and pivot as needed.

So far, I've been able to sustain and continue to grow through the first 3 years of being a full-time entrepreneur and surviving a worldwide pandemic, all because of being strategic in my planning, not allowing the success of others to derail me, taking care of myself, knowing when to pivot, taking leaps of faith and leaning on my support system. I know that my business is still young, but each day I am learning what it needs for continued growth. I am also learning to trust the process, knowing that everything works out the way it's supposed to in the end, and sometimes there are surprises along the way that you never expected that might help broaden your vision.

Some additional things I've learned in this process is that you have to be open to the unexpected. Every idea you have for your business may not reach its full potential; and that the rejection you receive, isn't always a hard "No", sometimes it just means, "Now is not the time". I've personally had many ideas that I really wanted to work on, some were successful and some did not flourish the way I'd hoped. However, it hasn't stopped me from creating my vision, adapting to the changes, and reimagining how I see my business growing.

You will also meet people along the way who might try to discredit your ability or try to derail you from your journey or question some of the decisions that you make. Embrace all the hurdles because you are the only one that can provide the world with the gifts that you were given.

As a woman, I would encourage you to create a network for yourself and/or get a mentor who's successfully been doing what you want to do. Having someone you can lean on during hurdles will be important for your journey because there will be enough naysayers so having support is a must. They will challenge you to push yourself but also remain true to yourself. They will also encourage you to think outside of the box and go BIG. My mentor is a boss in the field and she's helped me to see that the possibilities are endless. She is just a good human being and an awesome friend.

Another good practice is reading. Continue to educate yourself in your field and in the world of business. This is an essential part of helping you navigate some of the basics when it comes to owning and running a profitable business. You can read, "Profit First", by Mike Michalowicz. This book has been and continues to be critical in how I scale and grow my business. It is a huge reason I've been able to sustain during the pandemic. It helped me to get serious about putting systems in place and also outsourcing parts of my business that I did not need to do myself. I am not an expert at everything, but hiring people that know those areas of the business that I don't, is how I was able to double my income and why I am able to project more growth in the near future.

About Gretchen Campbell

GRETCHEN CAMPBELL is a Licensed Clinical Mental Health Counselor. She's an original Jersey girl but currently residing in Cary, North Carolina where she has been since 2009. Gretchen completed her undergraduate degree in Psychology at Kean University in Union, NJ, and her graduate degree in Counseling at Fairleigh Dickinson University located in Madison, New Jersey. She is the proud owner of Grow, Encourage, Empower a group therapy practice and growing wellness center in Cary, NC. She is passionate about the work that she does with the child and adolescent population as well as Generation Z and Millennials. She's a sought after speaker on all things teens as well as Mothers and Daughters and it is also the Best Selling Author of the debut book, I'm a Mom of a Teen Girl, Help that premiered in 2019, where she provides practical tools for mothers of teenage girls to implement during the sometimes rough developmental stage. She's a daughter, sister, and friend too many and passionate about helping others. Be on the lookout for more ventures to come, including her podcast, I'm a mom of Teen, Help as well as a budding community Brown Girlz Do that will assist brown girls connecting both on and offline.

Find Gretchen online at:

- https://www.instagram.com/gretchen_campbell_lcmhc/
- https://www.instagram.com/growencourageempower/
- https://twitter.com/GrowEncourage
- linkedin.com/in/gretchen-a-campbell-48200426/
- https://www.facebook.com/Growencourageempower
- https://www.amazon.com/Im-Mom-Teen-Girl-Help/dp/1733411909

"

In all my work, what I try to say is that as human beings we are more alike than we are unalike.

–Maya Angelou

God's Sense of Humor

by Sundrae "Sunny" Miller

Owning and operating a spa, "Adara", is my second career. It actually began as a side gig while working my original career, as a television news producer. Strange thing, I never knew doing nails was going to be a career. I just thought of it as a hobby, something I enjoyed doing while working in the grueling world of television. It's funny how life happens when you are busy making other plans. I always say, "God has a sense of humor". He is a comedian.

In 2001, after 12 years of working as a television news producer, I decided to call it quits. However, the Regional Emmy Awards were slated for just a few months after my departure, so I submitted an entry as my last hurrah. Although I hoped I'd win, I really didn't think I would. Lo and behold, I did! Sunny Miller was the winner of a Regional Emmy Award that now sits on my fireplace mantle.

As soon as that happened, people started asking if I was returning to the television station. I know leaving to do nails was a bold and risky move. Was I crazy? Some people were ready to bet money on it. However, the reality was that I was not crazy, just BURNED OUT.

Tired of chasing the dollar bill.

What is the use of making money if you are never home to enjoy it with the people you are struggling beside to create a dream? So often, we are incentivized by money. As a child, we're told to find a career that's going to make us money. However, it's not often we're told to find a career that you love and pays well too.

I earned a great salary in television.

However, I was unable to enjoy it or the things it afforded me because I was always at work and when I was home, I was tired.

That person by my side is my husband, Xavier. He and I met in the 11th grade in 1983.

He is my rock. His faith in me is what allowed me to pursue my passion.

Again, God has a sense of humor.

Xavier and I thought we would have a houseful of kids, but God had other plans. We have no biological children but we also have no shortage of youngsters that we have been able to embrace in our lives. In fact, we are currently foster parents to an 8-year-old son Jermaine and unofficially adoptive parents to our 20-year-old daughter, Ajah, who lives with us. Before they came to live with us, Xavier and Adara were my primary focus. I do not know how to explain it but Adara is still important, but not in the same way. I guess the best way I could put it is that while it holds my attention, Adara is not my sole focus. Having children in your home is like having a magnifying glass on your life. I am better able to focus on what is really important; and while Adara is important, it is no longer the center of my universe. Ajah is taking business classes in college.

Watching me work hard to build Adara has given her some real-life experiences, like an unpaid internship.

Jermaine often asks why I am always working. As he matures, he will realize the importance of a good work ethic. My absence in the home is also showing him as a strong male role model because my husband is taking care of him equally with me.

When I first left television, I rented a chair at a nail salon before moving to a corner in a hair salon. It was no larger than a cubicle but it was all I needed.

It provided peace of mind (most of the time), except when there was some sort of drama. You know, there is this belief that a bunch of women cannot work together without drama. However, that is not true. In fact, that is the only rule I have at Adara. NO DRAMA! If I wanted drama, I could have stayed at the television station. I learned while working in television, the person at the top sets the tone and atmosphere for the entire crew and set. Tension and attitude in the headsets trickle through the studio to each person on the headsets, like electricity traveling through a telephone line. Therefore, I have made it my mission as a spa owner to keep my attitude in check even when I am not having a stellar day. No one has the right to infringe on someone else's mood because she or he is having a bad day.

That is a philosophy I live by and embrace 100 percent.

Just as it takes a village to raise a child, as I am learning firsthand as a foster mom, it also takes a village to run, operate, and maintain a successful business. When the business came to a halt due to the world pandemic in 2020, COVID-19, I immersed myself in knowledge. I read more than I ever have. I subscribed to Forbes Magazine, Black Enterprise, the city newsletter, and any group I think will have helpful information. I connected with other business leaders. I also attended and participated in webinars. My sister has a saying, "How do you know what you know? You learn it for yourself." I would personally add that there is a subject you feel you cannot learn and master, hire a team of experts like most presidents. I have a great accountant, bookkeeper, and lawyer. Some of those relationships started with bartering until I could afford to pay for their services.

I remember when I first started out trying to make ends meet. I remember telling my accountant, I wanted to take home a thousand-dollar paycheck every week. Surprise, surprise; that did not last long. Reality slapped me in the face real quick. Although I did not take business classes, I have one of those types A personalities, I get things done! For example, when I was in my 20's, I would sit at my computer for hours looking for a missing penny in Quicken my bookkeeping software. Whoever knew that would come in handy. I did not realize I was learning how to budget and be prudent with every cent.

With the perspective of 20/20 hindsight, I should have probably majored in business instead of mass communications when I went to college. At least that is what I like to tell myself.

Fast forward to 2005, I managed to get my start with a loan from the Small Business Administration (SBA) thanks to attending a meeting at the Women's Business Center. The day I visited, there was a woman there showing attendees how to properly fill out the SBA application. She walked us through each question and explained how to best answer the questions. As a result, I received my first $15,000 loan. Over the years, I still needed operating capital and raised it by asking a select few clients to pre-pay for services. In exchange, they received 20 percent off until the balance was depleted.

I did not ask everyone because I still needed money daily. It worked well and sometimes I still offer that incentive to some clients when it looks like times are going to be tight.

Pre-paying has helped us weather the COVID-19 storm. Like many businesses, in order to prevent the further spread of the disease, we had to close the spa for 2 months to protect the public. Since reopening, the spa is only functioning at 50 percent.

I had to take on a new part-time job, while also finding grants online that are available. Do not let the word "grant" scare you. Applying for private grants is not the same as applying for a government grant. I have found that many of the applications require the same information. So hang on to your documentation and steer away from grants that ask for payment. Not all grants are created equal. Be sure to look at the eligibility and document requirements. Some grants are from reputable groups and others are not.

Do your homework! I am amazed at the number of people who will not seek out grants. The reasons vary and I think they are all foundationless. For example, "I do not know if I qualify. My taxes are not paid. I do not need it". And just for the record, you may not need a grant at this very moment, but who knows if we will have around two of COVID-19. And for those of you who say, I do not want to deprive someone who may need a grant more than me, there is no guarantee someone who needs it more than you is going to get it. Think about it, wouldn't it be great if you were in a position to help someone? That is what grants will allow me to do. I can sturdy up Adara's foundation while helping others. I have been able to hire a new full-time employee. I am also able to contribute, not much but something, to organizations close to my heart.

I often say, "I do not know why I named Adara a spa when all I did was nails and esthetics". I remember my interview with the first person I ultimately hired. I did a pedicure for her during the interview. I remember telling the young lady I did not need a massage therapist. By the time I had completed the pedicure, I remember asking, "When do you want to start?" Then I added another esthetician and a nail technician. For 10 years and 364 days, Adara was housed in a 900 square foot space, on the third floor of an office building with no signage. However, we did big things in that small space and clients walked out happy and satisfied. I knew I would not be happy until I could find a bigger and better location. Then my hand was forced. It came to my attention that the owners of the building were planning to sell. So, my quest began to find a new location.

That is when a client told me about a house for sale around the corner. I thought no way could I afford to buy a house in this neighborhood. As she watched me, I stared blankly at her, picked up the phone, left a message for the owner, and never expected anything to become of that call.

It was a dream of mine to own the building where Adara was housed. Acquiring the property that now houses Adara was a journey that strengthened my faith. Each time a door closed, a window cracked. But in order to do so, we needed the down payment. I first needed someone to see my vision, believe in me, and be willing to take a risk on me. That person was the banker at a community bank. She said yes when all the big box banks said no.

Once she gave me the go-ahead, I felt confident in borrowing the down payment. On the day of closing, the person who was loaning the money decided she was only going to give $35,000 instead of the $60,000 promised. Thank God for people who know your character, have witnessed your hard work, and believe in you because it is those people who will see you through to the end.

That was just the beginning of the hurdles I had to jump over to accomplish my dream. Next, there was the matter of too few parking spaces. The city ordinance changed just weeks after we purchased, helping us overcome that obstacle. Next, the biggest hurdle was the building not being zoned properly and not up to code. So, think of it this way. If your local leaders decide to zone your neighborhood residential and commercial, you could have houses beside businesses. So the zoning works. However, if you want to transform your house into a bed and breakfast, you might need to make sure your house is up to code… equipped with handicapped parking, a wheelchair ramp, wheelchair-accessible bathrooms, etc. Well, overlooking that little detail cost me $40,000 and 6 months of renovations that I didn't account for. Did I mention that we did not have the down payment? Again, thank God for people who believed in my dream and were willing to take a risk on it. Fortunately, I was able to refinance a few years down the road and repay everyone who loaned money.

My goal before COVID-19 was to hire staff that would allow me to step away from the chair and really oversee the future of Adara.

We were making strides in that direction but COVID-19 has created a temporary detour. I am not giving up on that dream or should I say, I am not giving up on my exit strategy. So often, I have heard of business owners just turning off the lights, flipping the closed sign, and walking away from it all. I want to have a sellable business that supports me in my retirement.

Adara is home to a diverse staff of nearly one dozen men and women (many independent contractors) ranging in age from 27 to 57, various ethnicities, and sexual identities. The success of Adara impacts all of these individuals and their livelihood.

Adara is like the "Cheers" of the beauty industry. Adara is where everyone knows your name. One of the hardest things for me since COVID-19 is not being able to hug my clients.

There is nothing like the human touch, and boy, do I miss it! Being at Adara's is like hanging out with friends all day. I tell the staff, we are not performing brain surgery. Therefore, our goal is to help guests forget about what is happening outside these four walls, if only for an hour. We are hanging out with friends and if they are having fun, we should too. That is evident by the fact that we were nominated for Best Day Spa in Raleigh, NC. I had no idea Adara was nominated as Best Day Spa in Raleigh, NC. In fact, you had to have a certain number of nominations to even make it to voting.

As it turned out, we were up against a spa and a medical spa both of which were big money establishments. It was an honor and frightening because I knew both places charged big money and appeared to have more access to funds.

In the end, none of that mattered.

Customer service was the key.

Adara won!!! Yay for the little guy.

As I have always said, God has a sense of humor. My entire journey is filled with His ironies. I am sure has chuckled along the way, waiting to see how I would handle the latest curveball he threw my way. You could have never told me that a little girl from South St Petersburg, FL would grow up to have a successful career in television and one day run her own business.

None of this was in my plans. At one point in my life, I believed that if I made it out of the projects and got my own apartment, I would have arrived.

That would have been the pinnacle of my success. Thank goodness God does not leave us to our own devices because I would have sold myself short. Thank God for His biggest blessing, the people He has placed in my life along this journey.

About Sundrae "Sunny" Miller

For 12 years, I worked in broadcast news in and around Florida's Tampa Bay area and Raleigh, North Carolina, and surrounding areas. Writing and reporting local, national, and international news was an exciting and always changing field. I even won an Emmy Award in 2001!

However, I wanted to expand on my communications and interpersonal skills. As a television news producer, I often found myself behind a desk and unable to interact with the public.

My career as a spa owner gives me the best of both worlds. Although my days are usually spent in the office, I am fortunate and blessed to connect with wonderful people from all different walks of life. I get to visit with friends daily while providing pampering and beauty services. My spa, Adara, offers everything from massages, facials, waxing, manicures, and pedicures. As a licensed esthetician and manicurist, I also provide hands-on skincare and body services. Plus, I have the opportunity to use my creative writing and marketing skills, in addition to, working as a national trainer for Light Concept Nails USA.

Find her online at:

https://www.adaraspa.com/about-us/sundrae-miller/

"

There is no such thing as failure.
Failure is just life trying to move us
in another direction.

−Oprah Winfrey

Rewards of Pouring Education into Others

by Ilka Huntley McElveen

Hello World! I am Ilka Huntley McElveen, granddaughter of an Aggie trailblazer, Esther Huntley, still going strong at 99 years young. I was born in Manhattan, NY on December 7, 1969, to Micheline Huntley, who was a teen mother, at the time. My father has been absent my entire life, just connecting with me three years ago when my grandfather passed. My grandmother raised me so my mother could attend North Carolina Agricultural & Technical State University, obtain her degree, and become self-sufficient to be able to take care of us both. Little did any of us know, this custodial setup would be the game-changer for my life.

Fast forward to the move from New York to North Carolina when I was four years old. My grandmother raised me with the help of my Aunt, Karen Huntley Kellam, while my mother and her twin; Frances Huntley Cooper attended and graduated from NCA&TSU with degrees in Education and Social Work. While my mother began her career as a Kindergarten Teacher in the county, I stayed with my grandmother. My grandmother built Rainbow Nursery School from the ground up in a cornfield in 1957. Her center was the only licensed childcare facility in Bladen County serving newborns to 12-year-olds of all races for over 15-20 years. She exposed families to travel, arts, and politics, giving back to the community in so many ways. She was elected to City Council, where she always put the community first.

In her center, we were offered jazz classes and piano lessons visited museums, lakes, beaches, mountains, and had guest speakers at the center. We even met Ella Fitzgerald. I remember growing up in the daycare center. We lived in one part and the other two rooms were for childcare. My grandmother is and always will be my 1st role model. I watched her give so much to so many families while helping them to make a better life for themselves. She encouraged education all of the time. Two of her favorite sayings were, "They can't take out what's in your brain; get an education so you can take care of yourself" and "Make every moment a teachable moment!"

Between the 10th and 11th grade of high school, my mother moved to Okinawa, Japan to teach for the Department of Defense as a Kindergarten teacher. I was very proud of her but I chose to only visit her during the summers because I didn't want to leave my grandmother. By this time, my grandmother and I had an "unbreakable bond." I was her travel buddy and her political sidekick attending conferences and traveling the country with her representing the child care center or our small country town of Elizabethtown. At 18, I traveled to China on a 14-day World Trade Mission with The World Conference of Mayors, along with my grandmother, Aunt Karen, and 1st cousin, Akil Huntley Cooper. During HS, I also cheered, drove the school bus, and worked at my grandmother's center. I was always an Honors Student and school was rather easy for me because I had great study skills, never procrastinated, and always asked questions when I was unsure.

Upon graduating High School, I attended NCA&TSU for one year. I moved back home, married my best friend and high school sweetheart, Freddie McElveen, Jr. whom I met while working at McDonald's. After eloping in 1989, at the young age of 19, I worked at a local turkey plant in production for four days and came to the realization I did not want to spend my life working in a plant. I knew I had a purpose but had not quite found it yet. For about 18 months, I juggled working at CVS, driving a school bus, and working at my grandmother's center. My husband worked at a local plant and was enlisted in the Army National Guard Reserves. We welcomed our 1st born, Freddrianna McElveen on November 24, 1991, after a miscarriage. We were elated, especially because I was told in middle school I would never be able to carry a baby to term due to my scoliosis. I wore a brace for 23 hours a day during my 7th and 8th-grade years of school.

Since we were starting our family, my grandmother urged my husband to pursue a trade since he wasn't interested in going to school for a degree. So he went to barbering school. He graduated from DZ Barber College, Spring Lake, NC in 1992 as a Licensed Barber. This would be his trade for the next 26 years. In January 1992, with Freddrianna being just 6 weeks old, I re-enrolled in college and became a full-time, nontraditional, off-campus student at Fayetteville State University, commuting one hour, one way daily to and from classes, while Freddrianna would spend her days in the center with my family. I still helped out at the center, but my hands were full with a new baby, full-time classes, husband, and the 2 hours drive each day. I breastfed her and pumped to provide bottles when I was in class, which was a lot of work and very tiring.

So many days I couldn't tell if I was coming or going, sleepless nights, staying up studying, and preparing for her baby needs the next day: bibs, changes of clothes, bottles, pampers, baby bags, etc. I took her to class with me some days because her pediatrician was in Fayetteville and my husband was working. Those days were the toughest and I felt like giving up. I remember being on the production line at the turkey plant, knowing I wanted to do so much more for my daughter. That's why I was determined to finish college this time, making the Dean's List each semester. However, I took the fall semester off in 1993, when I became pregnant with baby #2. On November 2, 1993, we welcomed our daughter, Myesha McElveen, into the world. We were full of joy with our new addition! This time, Freddrianna would continue to attend the daycare, sharing a special bond with my Aunt Karen. Conveniently, my grandmother lived with us, at the time, and would keep Myesha at our home while I went back to the full-time grind as a student.

Still determined, with more people depending on me now than before. My major was Elementary Education when I gave birth to Myesha; but when an ENT specialist told me she may never speak, I changed my major to Speech. I was not accepting that as an outcome, so I had a little talk with Jesus. Then, I began helping her with phonetics, enunciation, and pronunciation; and today, no one would ever imagine she was born with speech delays. I continued on my educational journey, finding out in the spring of 1996, I was pregnant again with baby number 3. I pressed my way through morning sickness, with teachers allowing me to chew gum in class because it helped with nausea. On November 21, 1996, I gave birth to our 3rd daughter, Tavonda McElveen, with the thankful heart of another healthy baby. On December 14, 1996, while our newest blessing, Tavonda was just 23 days old; I marched across the stage and received my BA Degree in Speech/Theater with Honors. My family celebrated with me; my mother flew in from Okinawa, Japan; my grandmother, my great grandmother, Margaret McNeill, my husband, and the girls were all there supporting me. I was so proud of myself. I was thankful to God for allowing me to safely make that commute for 3 and a half years, some days with no sleep at all. I had a goal set and I achieved it!

With that being said, I don't want to hear the excuses of young girls telling me they can't go to the local community college to earn their degree. If God helped me, he will help them, IF they are willing to put the time in and work. Of course, it may not be easy, but it is obtainable. If I could do it with three babies, a husband, and working, they can do it too.

Upon graduating college, I interviewed for a position at American Express and was offered a 6-figure income. I turned it down because my husband did not want to relocate. I was devastated, but I knew my grandmother also needed me, so I ended up working for her. It was convenient and important to be with my girls in the early years of their learning. I became Director of the center; but as my grandmother began to age, she didn't want to release the center to me 100 percent as recommended by the State. During this time, I became pregnant with baby number 4. This pregnancy was like no other. With the stress of life and the challenges of "trying to make grandmother happy plus do the right thing for my family", I suffered a miscarriage at 8 weeks, on Super Bowl Sunday 1999. Doctors refused to do a D & C, stating I was still pregnant. In my mind, there was no way this could have been true. I was released and put on bed rest.

Twenty-four weeks later, my water started to leak, and I gave birth 3 months early on June 29, 1999, to our angel Hadiyah McElveen. Hadiyah was born with 4 heart defects at 27 weeks gestation, weighing 2lbs 2oz. She was one of the multiples, but the others had miscarried. She was treated at Cape Fear Valley Medical Center in Fayetteville, NC and when her PDA didn't close, she was airlifted to UNC-Chapel Hill Children's Hospital NICU on the 4th of July. She lived a few more days, and then passed away after 5-hour heart surgery.

During our hospital stay, as the doctors were telling us of her prognosis and the poor quality of life she would have, I had another little talk with Jesus. I spoke to God as if he was sitting right in front of me and told him, "God if you're not going to heal her and if what the doctors are saying about her quality of life is true, please take her. I don't want her here on earth suffering with surgery after surgery, not being able to participate in playing with others, and even working up a sweat to feed herself!" I know to some it may seem selfish of me, but she was very sick. She passed on the morning of July 15 at exactly 2 weeks old.

We did a small graveside for her and it was the closure I needed. Everything just happened so fast.

My family and I were not on good terms, so I left my grandmother with her center. My husband and I opened our own center right around the corner. Grandmother became a competition. This was a very uneasy time for me; still grieving, and the family seemed to be falling apart because of the tension between us. On October 30, 2000, we welcomed our first son, Tyrese McElveen, after 4 daughters. Happy hearts again and the family seemed to be pulling together because of the new addition. Eventually, my grandmother conceded, realizing she needed my assistance, and gave me the deed to her land and building. We didn't jump on the opportunity right away. The building remained vacant for a few years. We welcomed daughter number 5, Tatianna McElveen, on September 11, 2003, and our 2nd son, Jair McElveen on December 26, 2005. We were overflowing with enthusiasm as our family had grown.

During this time we focused on our family and our business. We moved back to my grandmother's center in 2009 and closed it in 2011. I was burnt out working with children. Our oldest daughter was in her 2nd year of college and needed money for an International Honors Trip to Ghana from NCA&TSU. The proceeds from selling the daycare items helped her get to Ghana. While the center was closed, motivated by my children and trying to be the best educational role model possible, I enrolled in the Distance Learning Graduate Program at NCA&TSU. While I was taking a break from working with children, I worked at Smithfield Foods in Tar Heel, NC.

I started in production, and after a few weeks, I was hired as Quality Assurance Tech One. This was a salaried position, with 11 inspectors under my supervision. God heard my cry and moved me! This was an amazing job, with extraordinary people. I felt my purpose was to keep the food (Rib Line) safe for consumption and I took my job very seriously. I didn't want anyone getting sick or getting bad meat on my watch. I learned so much about the agriculture industry, and on May 12, 2012, I graduated with an MS in Agricultural Education, Summa Cum Laude. This was another proud moment of my determination to succeed, and once again, my family was my biggest supporter.

Not feeling complete and wanting to keep going, I earned an OSHA Certification in 2013. In March 2013, I reopened my grandmother's building as Kidz N Motion Child Care Center, using my Capstone Graduate Project as a guide. Our center was the first in NC to offer children elliptical equipment, teaching line dances to young children, and yoga as part of a campaign to raise awareness in healthier living. If they learn to exercise as a youth, they may continue into adult life and live longer healthier lives.

On February 15, 2014, we had our "surprise" finale baby, our 3rd son, Saeed McElveen. I was 44 years old. Oh, how our hearts were so full. We now had 7 children. For me, that was a sign of completion from God.

My entire life (50 years) has revolved around children in childcare, as a bus driver, community teens, and my own children. Kidz N Motion Child Care Center serves children from the age of newborn to 12 years. Many, not all, of our families, receive subsidy vouchers for payment assistance from the Department of Social Services. We provide care for many single-parent working families, as well. Our client's become family to us. My staff and I have a very personal and close relationship with each of our families. This makes the job much easier as caregivers and the parents are more comfortable leaving their children with us.

Since we serve more low-income families, we fundraise often to do annual family trips to Disney. We offer and encourage local family group trips to Myrtle Beach, Pirates Voyage, Riverbanks Zoo, Columbia SC, UniverSoul Circus, Disney On Ice, and Hockey Games in Fayetteville, NC before COVID19 hit. We have offered the 2nd shift and after-hours care for parents working two jobs or going to school at night.

Many events I would like to expose my own children to, I extend the invitation to the center families, as well.

I have witnessed and learned over the years, you must be responsible for your own actions. No one has the same "love for your business" as you do. I'm not saying others do not care for your business, because I have an amazing group of loyal and dedicated staff that I would not be able to operate my center if it were not for them. They know what is expected; they do their job very well. If you don't have a great team or staff, reaching your goals will be harder to attain but not impossible. As a business owner, it is important to keep an open mind. Grasp opportunities that may be challenging, because sometimes there are blessings in the strangest places.

As an entrepreneur, wife, and mother of 7 children, it has been a fun, often stressful, yet very rewarding journey. When my children were younger, I had to be organized. On Sundays, I would iron 5 outfits a piece for each child; make sandwiches for the week (freezing them and labeling them), washing hair, and putting hair bow colors to match the outfits. I would always keep a change of clothes in my vehicle for my younger children. As they got older, they each helped with their younger siblings so it made life easier for me.

Now, I am proud to say my oldest is Dr. Freddrianna McElveen, DVM, married to Trent Martin, with our 1st and only grandchild, Gabriel Martin. My 2nd oldest, Myesha McElveen Cooper, is about to graduate with a Master's in Human Resources, married to Gerald Cooper. The 3rd oldest, Tavonda McElveen, has a BS in Animal Science and is a teacher at a local military academy. Tyrese McElveen, our 1st son, is a sophomore at NCA&TSU majoring in Animal Science, as well. My other three children are still home and have been very helpful during virtual learning. Tatianna and Jair help the youngest, Saeed, with his online work. Tatianna, our math whiz, cheered until COVID-19 ended that;

and Jair just completed one year after being elected as the NC Jr. Beta President for the entire state of NC.

It is hard to juggle family and business life, especially when you have children who are involved in so much. That's when you solicit help from family and friends for a pick-up, drop-off, carpooling, and Uber services so you don't run yourself thin. My children have been successful in their own journeys, and I am an extremely proud parent of them all. They have made many sacrifices, along with my husband and me, to make the center work. Some days it was just my children and I look after the children who came to the center. Then other days, it was my husband and me. You must have a good support team and I am thankful that I do.

As a business owner, I recalled many ways my grandmother operated her business. Some of her tactics I apply to the center now, but some, I didn't. When times are changing, we must change. What worked years ago, may not work now. I have learned through the years to be friendly, but it's not always a good idea to hire friends. They either get upset when you expect them to do the required job duties or they don't take their responsibilities seriously.

When I started as a Director, I was placed in that position as a convenience and as assistance to my grandmother. Honestly, I had no goals set. I was young and didn't want to run the center because Speech Pathology was my dream, and childcare was my grandmother's dream. In appreciation for all she had done for me, I accepted the position and learned the business. As I have matured, I see the rewards of pouring education, nourishment, and dedication into the children. It is a good feeling and place to be. We have graduated doctors, judges, lawyers, mechanics, teachers, preachers, engineers, supervisors, and the list goes on. This is a huge accomplishment in the African American community because the foundation instilled at the center aided in keeping these children on the right track to become successful citizens of the community. Many of them give back to the youth now, as we gave to them.

My goals now are to take what my grandmother did to the next level and I am on the road to accomplishing that. Where she had to rent a bus to take the children on trips, we have fundraised and purchased our own buses. Where she didn't have the Internet, we have WIFI, offering virtual learning for those who are not attending school now due to COVID-19. We even purchased tablets, computers, and Google Hub Max's for each classroom, introducing our infants to technology with age-appropriate activities.

Today, with the help of grants such as the one offered by HerSuiteSpot, we are thankful we have been able to keep our business afloat. When COVID19 hit, we were unsure for about 18 weeks because only a handful of our children attended. So I placed staff on part-time hours with full-time pay, plus bonuses, so they wouldn't have to sign up for unemployment. When some of the executive orders were lifted, we began to see an increase in enrollment. We are now almost at capacity. Like many other businesses, I don't know what we would have done without the help of people like Marsha Guerrier, Founder of HerSuiteSpot to help Women on the Rise.

My journey has not been an easy one. I've suffered losses and experienced unexplainable euphoria, as you have read my story. I know if my grandmother had not taken me under her wing, I would not be the "game-changer" I am today. My mother was active in my life, but her being overseas, made me want to be that "overly active" parent in my own children's lives. In turn, I became somewhat of the "community" mother because if I didn't have daycare children, I had my children's friends with me.

If I can offer this one piece of advice to any entrepreneur, "Always remember your vision is your vision. No one will do what you expect to be done as you would or exactly like you because it is not their vision. Have patience with people, but be clear about how you want them to navigate and be an asset to you, your business, and your clients." At the end of the day, they go home; you're still the business owner. Don't be afraid to share your story when others offer excuses as to why they can't do this or that. Sometimes we need to let folks know we had a struggle too. Nothing is handed to you that you don't work for. You will also appreciate it better when you've worked hard for it.

About Ilka Huntley McElveen

When life hands you lemons, you make lemonade and positively change the world!

Cut from a very different cloth, as a Wife, Mother, Caregiver of an aging grandmother, Child Care Provider, Youth & Community Advocate, and the list goes on, I run tirelessly for my family, my business, and my community.

Inheriting the family child care business established 63 years ago, my greatest passion is creating a place of refuge for the children & families of whom I provide care for. I help my families with more than just child care, I offer family events and annual trips being many of our children have never been out of the county. The majority of our children come from single-parent households, so we encourage the parents to re-enroll in school, obtain a degree or certification to be able to provide a better life for themselves and their children.

Our youth and community are important. Our center hosts youth events as well as takes "at-risk" youth on weekend trips. I help local businesses in the community with grant and loan applications to assist in starting a new or growing an existing business in the community. Helping others positively change the world and their lives for the better.

My educational background includes an MS Agriculture Education and OSHA Certification from North Carolina Agricultural & Technical State University in Greensboro, NC. I have a BA in Speech/Theater minor from Fayetteville State University, Fayetteville, NC.

Find her online at:

http://m.facebook.com/Kidz-N-Motion-781277425311838/

"

*If they don't give you a seat at the
table, bring a folding chair.*

– Shirley Chisholm

A Parable of Healing

by Dr. Jennifer Pierre

At the age of 13, I confidently declared I would become a physician. In my mind, there was no reason why I could not be - I was smart, focused and a lifelong honor roll student. Prior to that declaration, I wanted to be a nurse like my mom. I had numerous experiences of accompanying mom at Hempstead General Hospital or at Peninsula Hospital Center where dad worked as a lab technologist. I enjoyed identifying various strains of bacteria in a microscope. In ninth grade biology lab, I dissected a frog; there was such joy in my heart upon gleaning what was inside! In high school, I committed to caring for a friend's infected ear piercing. It healed as good as new. I was certain my destiny was to become a surgeon.

In Haitian culture, there are only three careers that exist: lawyer, doctor, or engineer, so I was definitely on the right track as far as my parents were concerned. I later learned this cultural norm was similar for many other immigrant children. My parents migrated from Haiti at the height of the "Baby Doc" dictatorship. My dad, one of twelve, was very intelligent, known by his teachers as a math and science wiz. In Haiti, he completed studies to become a lawyer, but when he came to the states, his degree was not recognized. Back home, he was a brilliant promising young man who decided to buck the status quo, which proved dangerous for many others. His parents sent him to the states to further his education and remove him from an environment that was limited by the political structure. I am well aware that my ability to choose my career was a privilege. I got to decide what I wanted to be, while my father's trajectory was decided for him. My Mom is the creative and the nurturer. She is extremely clever and quick-witted. When she first came to America, she worked as a seamstress but aspired to become a nurse. In middle school, I watched her grow her career from a nurse's aide to a licensed practical nurse. She is the most selfless person I know. She is one of my biggest cheerleaders and a BOSS. The combination of my parental units contributed to my traits of tenacity, organization, diligence, and discipline, which I believe are vital as an entrepreneur.

Growing up, it was hard to find a physician who dealt with preventative care. I remember hearing about those old-school doctors who spent time with you and some even went to people's homes. In contrast, my annual visit with my pediatrician was 15 minutes in and out. When I was 15, I had a recurring female issue. My mother took me to her gynecologist to figure out what was wrong. After the third occurrence, I asked him if there were any ways to prevent it. He deflected from the question and just told me to keep taking the prescribed medication. Now there was already a power dynamic that made it hard to speak up, but curiosity got the better of me. Even as a teenager it made no sense to me to keep taking this medication that was known to damage the liver over time. So I started doing research on my own. To give you some context, this was the 90s, way before the Google search engine.

I had to go get actual books at the library (insert Generation Z scream.) The more I learned, the more I knew there was more to learn.

Consequently, at an early age, I became very health conscious.

At 16, I had no idea that choosing Cornell University for college would be one of the best decisions I would ever make.

Cornell led me to a destiny entwined with my now husband and my best friend for life. I was a pre-med student majoring in biology when I realized that I did not want to go the conventional route. Being at an Ivy League school institution, I was afforded the best pre-medical education and opportunities to shadow medical doctors at Weill Cornell Medical Center in New York City.

At 19 years old, I had a fundamental issue with the lack of time spent with patients and the focus on pharmaceutical drugs in those experiences and in conventional medical school education. So I made the decision to no longer pursue medicine. I was heartbroken and confused, not knowing what to do next.

When I told my father, the reality of that decision truly set in and created a rift that would take years to mend.

Thankfully, one of my friends presented me with the idea to study public health. The more I learned about it, the more it fell in line with my ethos of preventive medicine. I began taking classes that focused on population dynamics, gender equality, and health equity. I was excited about school again and thrived in my new major Development Sociology.

After graduation, I began coursework at SUNY Albany School of Public Health. Public Health was flexible and wide-reaching, allowing me to study several aspects of healthcare at the same time. My focus was on biomedical sciences and community health. I felt like I was on my path, as this was the closest thing to preventive medicine at a systems level, aiming to address health equity concerns. During my master's program, I learned about the American healthcare system's shift from natural medicine to consumer-driven medicine in the early 20th century. I felt duped and it all started to make sense. It upset me that profit came before wellness. To make matters worse, at age 22, I found out scoliosis was responsible for the chronic back pain I had suffered for years. Those 15-minute annual pediatrician visits were to blame for my missed diagnosis; unfortunately, it was too late to do anything about it. It only strengthened my desire for a preventive integrative health care system.

My career in public health consisted of various roles including prenatal health educator, health workforce and geriatrics researcher, and mental health counselor. Yet, I still yearned for more. I always felt that I was being spiritually led to a deeper type of healing. In my 20s, I traveled the world, developed a love of health and fitness, and entertained other professions: a model, natural hair blogger, and even went to India to become a yoga instructor. All the while searching for medicine I never knew existed - naturopathic medicine.

Integrative Medicine is a Part of Who I Am

Natural medicine (referred to as complementary or alternative medicine in the Western world) has been used throughout many cultures for centuries. Most of the pharmaceutical drugs we hold dear are synthetic derivatives of the plants that were commonly used in the ancient cultures of America, Africa, and Asia.

Growing up Haitian, natural and conventional medicine peacefully coexisted. My grandfathers on both sides were farmers from L'Artibonite, a rural area in the middle of the country two hours from the capital, Port au Prince.

This river valley was the agricultural hub of Haiti and grew most of the produce fueling our strong penchant for rice.

In some of the rural areas of Haiti, conventional doctors are few and far between. Local medicine men and women serve as the lifeline for these villages - even today.

In my 20s, I adored Barnes and Noble and would sit on the floor of the health or self-help section for hours. I started learning more about nutrients and the benefit of herbs, which prompted me to start shopping at local health food stores.

One day while perusing supplements at The Vitamin Shoppe, I discovered a book called "Prescriptions for Natural Healing". Years later as a manager, VS would become the driving impetus for going to naturopathic medical school. I read the book from cover to cover; it became my natural health resource. I began daydreaming about the day I would open up my own integrative wellness center.

What the Heck is a Naturopathic Doctor?

I am so glad that you asked! Naturopathic Doctors (NDs) must complete 4-5 years at an accredited naturopathic medical school. During that time, naturopathic medical students study the same basic and clinical sciences as a conventional medical doctor. At the same time, natural treatments are incorporated into the curriculum. These modalities include botanical medicine, Chinese medicine, acupuncture, hydrotherapy, homeopathy, and physical medicine. NDs in training also learn clinical nutrition, IV therapy, minor surgery, and mind-body medicine - in other words - #nodaysoff. Prior to state licensure, two sets of professional board examinations must be successfully completed. As a result, NDs are trained as primary care physicians (PCPs), but many specialize in certain areas like endocrinology, pediatrics, or oncology.

Depending on the state licensure, NDs can practice as PCPs or specialists. For example: in Connecticut, I am considered a specialist, while in Arizona I am a PCP.

I chose to go to naturopathic medical school in Arizona because it had the largest scope of practice in the country including prescriptive authority. I was drawn to the weather and health-conscious environment. I also wanted to challenge myself in a foreign environment.

In addition, my school Southwest College of Naturopathic Medicine (SCNM) was where Naturopaths Without Borders (NWB) was founded. Because of this, I was able to participate in medical missions in my beloved Haiti and Mexico. Medical school was hard, but Arizona was nurturing and it supported my mental well-being. The desert was the metaphor for my life. I moved to Arizona shortly after completing my yoga teacher training in India. I had become more adventurous and fully engrossed in my spiritual journey. Being so far away from home allowed me to take on this new foreign environment, make new friends, and tackle medical school. The desert challenged me. With my medical coursework, I could no longer keep up with my mornings of yoga and meditation, but being in Arizona was a perfect place to focus. I even found a church home, Faith Christian Center. FCC helped to sustain my spiritual growth in the desert. My four and a half years in Arizona was the perfect spiritual bridge between one life journey to the next.

The Calling Requires Sacrifice

Choosing the naturopathic path was not an easy one.

The current American healthcare model is reactionary and for profit. You have to have thick skin in this profession, because some medical professionals are threatened, confused, and even fearful of a prevention-based approach to medicine. You would not believe the lengths some people go to discredit naturopathic medicine. Further complicating the credibility issue of the naturopathic profession are individuals who study traditional naturopathy online at a non-accredited program, but use the "naturopathic doctor" title freely in pre-licensed states. While they are holistic practitioners, they are ineligible for state licensure. Any mistake they make is an affront to our entire profession because most people do not know the difference. There is danger in this as more and more people are so desperate for natural medicine they will go to anyone. Here is an important tip when looking for a healthcare provider: if you are ever in doubt about a physician's credentials, research where they went to medical school, look up their state license number and/or NPI number.

I knew that I would face marginalization as a naturopathic doctor, but when I explored the curriculum, it was everything I ever wanted to learn about medicine. I could not believe that a medical professional like this existed all this time and I never knew about it. Psychologically, it was hard to wrap my brain around going back to school again; it felt like starting over and I felt like I was losing my best years to school. But I kept receiving reminders that it was bigger than me. All those hours of meditation and prayer confirmed that this was my purpose and it was what I was instructed to do by God to heal others. It was my way of combining spirit and service in the embodiment of Christ's love through healthcare.

Outside of a licensed naturopathic doctor, there is no other licensed medical provider who studies both conventional and natural medicine in medical school. As a physician, my philosophy is integrative – a world where we integrate natural and conventional medicine together. Natural medicine is making a huge comeback due in part to the rise in chronic disease in the United States. Most of these diseases are preventable through diet and lifestyle changes. These include but are not limited to cardiovascular disease, diabetes, hypertension, hypercholesterolemia, and cancer. An effective way to decrease these rates is through patient education. I am passionate about educating people about the variety of treatment options available to them. Sometimes you need pharmaceutical drugs and sometimes you do not. If you are reading this and you desire an integrative physician that desires to get to the root cause of your condition, seek out a licensed naturopathic doctor. Check out naturo-pathic.org to learn more.

A Phoenix Rises As An Entrepreneur is Born

After leaving Arizona, I unexpectedly came back to the east coast. The original plan was to open up a naturopathic practice in Georgia with one of my classmates. But I fell in love with a fellow Cornellian and wound up practicing medicine in Connecticut. I started working for two medical practices. Each practice was a little different, so my patient base was different. I learned about the diversity (or lack thereof) of the two Connecticut counties.

I started studying how the practices were run and could not help but notice the inefficiencies of both. I have always been very observant, which is good or bad depending on who or what is on the other end. It became very hard to watch the inefficiencies and not work to improve them. In true Jen fashion, I went above and beyond. I built a solid patient base, but I grew disappointed at the lack of appreciation for my hard work. I decided to take steps in moving forward towards my dream of opening up a wellness center. In 2017, I registered my business JenteelNature LLC, which initially focused on public health consulting for local municipalities.

After two years of working at practice A, I tried to negotiate a higher fee split, but I was denied. This was significant because the owner had fallen seriously ill and during that time, I stepped up in helping to keep things afloat. The owner claimed she could not afford to increase my split. A few months later I put in my notice. Shortly thereafter, she offered that same increase to a male colleague who admitted that he too had contemplated leaving the practice. A few months after I left, I found out she regretted not giving me the larger split.

She missed out on making more money with a talented physician, who honestly should have asked for even more.

Meanwhile, at practice B, I had been promoted to Medical Director. That quickly turned into Chief Medical Officer as I handled everything, but the monthly bills. I was excited to take on my new role, but it was not for the faint of heart. The owners had undergone a messy divorce and practice management had taken a back seat. This was happening at the exact same time owner A had fallen ill and I was planning a wedding. Both practices were falling apart at the same time and I was overwhelmed. My first task was to hire a brand new staff of doctors and a new receptionist. God bless my husband Arthur who volunteered to help run operations part-time while in a full-time master's program at Yale University. His background in finance, community development, and running his own real estate business came in handy. We created a master list of former patients to contact. Hubby's melodic voice and charm wooed the patients back in, in the same way, that it helped him create valuable connections all throughout his life. But our next step was to create an infrastructure to keep them coming back.

Hiring and Firing

Probably the most important thing an entrepreneur can do for his or her business is to hire the right people. My first task at practice B was to hire a front desk person.

We really needed someone to answer the phones and create a welcoming environment for new and returning patients.

While on the hunt, one of my patients reached out to me expressing interest in the role. The first thing I noticed was her initiative. She was someone who knew what she wanted and went after it. In addition, she had years of experience in customer service as a hairstylist. As a fellow creative, I knew that trait would prove invaluable in a business. To this day, I say that was the best decision I made for practice B. The first hire sets the foundation for all other employees who will work for you. Over time, I have learned to hire slowly and fire quickly, albeit humanely. I always provide a 90-day probation period for both parties to determine fit. If it does not work out, either party is free to part ways.

Launching The JenteelNature Experience

I wanted to switch things up at practice B. First, I wanted to integrate the practice into the neighborhood. Although the practice had been there for over fifteen years, it was not inviting. Our plan was to revamp the look of the practice to bring it into the 21st century. After making these changes, we noticed more pedestrians stopping in to inquire about our services. Due to the racial makeup of New Haven, CT - approximately ⅓ Black, ⅓ Latinx, and ⅓ Caucasian, I wanted to build a practice of physicians who reflected that. The NDs I hired were diverse in ethnicity, specialty areas, smart, easy to work with, and possessed excellent bedside manner. Finally, we desperately needed to employ more technology. Before officially becoming CMO, I had already chosen an Electronic Medical Records System (EMR) fully equipped with automatic patient reminders, inventory, e-fax capability, and video conferencing. Prior to this, everything was paper-based, which was not very environmentally friendly, and terribly inefficient.

Next, we focused on our operations. I love organization; while that may have been an issue for others, it is extremely important in business. As it turns out, there were never any Standard Operating Procedures (SOPs) for either of these businesses. It did not seem to bother them; it was disconcerting. SOPs are critical for a successful business as it is important for operations to be carried out the same way every time.

The Push I Needed - Adios, Au revoir, Man, I'm out!

My mother once told me, it is human nature to get all you can from a person or situation. Many times it is unintentional, but in my case, it was not. There was no world where either practice owner would say, "Hey Dr. Pierre could you please stop making my medical practice better than it is?" I stepped up as a leader in both instances and was taken advantage of, as I was never properly compensated for my hard work. However, in the process, I discovered a new skill that I never knew I had - running a medical practice. Both practices were not life-giving for me, thereby affecting my philosophy of care and the experience I wanted my patients to have. So at the height of the 2020 Coronavirus pandemic, I left practice B.

My current business, JenteelNature Health is the culmination of my calling, twenty years in the making. Everything I set up for practice B has served me well in my own venture. JenteelNature Health provides telemedicine consults, public health, and corporate wellness consulting.

Public health programming improves health at the macro level, while telemedicine improves health at a micro-level (decreasing any physical limitations or barriers). My experience as both a naturopathic doctor and public health professional enables me to apply the principles I have learned to prevent disease, protect the health of the public and promote healthy lifestyles.

Navigating the Dual Pandemics

When the coronavirus hit, it was my public health training that alerted me this was going to have a huge long-term impact.

In school, we learned all about disaster preparedness and bioterrorism so it was shocking that there were no systems in place to contain the imminent threat. My ethos of prevention and preparation guided me through the most challenging period in modern American history. I already had systems in place to move to a virtual platform. Years earlier, I had toyed with the idea of telemedicine but had never gotten around to fleshing out all the details. I would soon learn that insurance reimbursement for telemedicine visits was half that of in-office visits. That would soon change as it became apparent that telemedicine was here to stay.

Telemedicine visits allowed patients to receive life-saving care. My pivot to telemedicine was one strategy that saved my business.

The pandemic revealed two public health crises at once - a deadly virus and systemic racism. Here you had political structures and a healthcare system that deemed a particular population of people unworthy. After the initial shock wore off, it became clear that it was Black people who were dying the most from COVID-19. I do not believe it was coincidental that when this was determined, the government and many American citizens were ready to open the country back up. Systemic racism and health inequities were not new to me. This is the same system that had revealed itself to me all those years ago; the same system that puts profit before healing.

Even public health has been reduced to mandatory vaccinations, but prevention and protecting the health of the public is so much more than that. No healthcare system is perfect, but this was where my philosophical conflict was highlighted yet again.

As I moved full force into entrepreneurship, I encountered barriers to funding my business. It is not uncommon that Black entrepreneurs lack the social, educational and financial capital to support a new business venture. As a virtual business, I was able to save money, but my patient load had decreased significantly. I began reaching out to local business development centers. I was amazed at all the services that were available for free. The Connecticut Women's Business Development Center (WBDC) was particularly helpful.

I also participated in two business cohorts during this time: The City of New Haven's DNA of an Entrepreneur and WBDC/Liberty Bank's Academy for Small Business. Once it was apparent that Black-owned businesses were bearing the brunt of the financial impact, more funding was made available. I received PPP and EIDL, but it became an additional job to apply for as many grants as I could. The HerRise Grant was the first grant that I received during the pandemic to support my business.

Niche Away

In my private practice, I was hesitant to niche even though my focus was always on women's health. I was that medical student that felt a sense of accomplishment upon locating the cervix on our mock patients in the gynecology lab (God bless those volunteers). Later on, in my medical school career, I would excel in my endocrinology shifts with actual patients. My supervising physicians began giving me all the hard cases. I worked hard, never wanting to disappoint them. I loved treating women's health concerns. I really admire the self-sacrificing nature of women, yet we do not often get care on par with that we give out. When you treat the matriarch of the family, everyone is better for it. It is a longstanding joke among physicians that if a male patient comes into your office, he was sent by his wife, girlfriend, mother, sister, or daughter.

Due to our lady parts, women have all types of issues that require a level of personal attention and amazing bedside manner. I treat women for all types of menstrual disorders and concerns that impact fertility including PMS, PMDD, PCOS, and fibroids (and I also treat women for that same issue I had all those years ago - naturally). It has come to my attention that Black and brown women are most disproportionately affected by these conditions that threaten their fertility outcomes. Unfortunately, these tend to be the same populations that cannot afford Assisted Reproductive Technology (ART). My husband and I have a non-profit entity Divine Grace Foundation that provides financial literacy, health education, mentoring and economic empowerment. Our plan is to acquire grants through our foundation to fund the medical services provided by JenteelNature Health for low-income populations. My goal is to be a thought leader in the health equity space.

My vision is to use preventative medicine to treat both individuals and communities to improve access to equitable quality healthcare.

On my journey thus far I have learned some valuable truths:

- Never doubt your calling.
- If you are struggling with identifying your purpose in life, investigate who you wanted to be when you were growing up.
- Move-in excellence always employing tenacity and resilience.
- Reinforce your passion and gift with formal training.
- Your team and operational structures should embody the ethos of your company.
- Sacrifice and consistency are part of your investment.
- Value those employees that work hard and strive to see your business succeed.

- Know your worth and add tax.
- Do not go above and beyond for people who take you for granted.
- Sometimes being taken for granted is the only thing that can force you to leave a place or situation that no longer serves you.
- Build authentic organic connections with your consumer.
- Place yourself in the role of your ideal customer, envision the experience you would want to have.
- Never stop learning to perfect your craft.
- Learn to identify trends early and pivot when necessary.
- Let love and service be your driving ethos.

It has been said that entrepreneurship is a marathon, not a sprint. I liken it more to a labyrinth. When you enter the maze, you think you know where you are going, only to encounter unexpected walls. The many twists and turns are dizzying. If fear sets in, you panic. If you take a moment, you start to recognize patterns that lead you to a pathway. A small part of you knows that you will find a way out if you use the skills you learned along the way; if you let fear take over, you miss the exit (i.e. the lesson). Are you the type of individual to give up when you hit those dark corners or do you keep going?

The hardest part of my journey has been keeping my mindset pure, and not falling into a spirit of helplessness. Without hope, you are already defeated. Hope leads to courage and courage leads to joy. The disappointments of the past have no place in your future - it can be different this time. When I look back, I acknowledge that I did not dream big enough. Now, I strive to have dreams that I can barely capture into my consciousness! I am optimistic about my future because I bet on myself and persevered in the middle of a worldwide pandemic! I am still in awe of that young woman who chose to live life differently and stood in her truth. She still holds a place in my psyche and I am reminded to stay the course and persist. On this entrepreneurial journey, stand strong in your truth and grab hold of a solid anchor. My anchor is God and "the plans He has for me". Be sure to hold onto your plans as well.

About Dr. Jennifer Pierre

Dr. Jennifer Pierre is the founder and CEO of JenteelNature Health, a boutique health consultancy.

As a physician and public health professional, she specializes in women's health, with the goal of improving reproductive health outcomes and reducing health disparities. Dr. Pierre integrates her knowledge of medicine with public health acumen by designing public health and wellness programs and provides medical advisory for non-profits and corporate entities. She has been voted 10Best in the Natural Nutmeg Readers' Choice Awards repeatedly.

Dr. Pierre is a licensed Naturopathic physician in Arizona and Connecticut. She received her Doctorate in Naturopathic Medicine from Southwest College of Naturopathic Medicine & Health Sciences in Tempe, Arizona. Dr. Pierre is a native New Yorker and alumna of Cornell University and University at Albany, School of Public Health. Her experience as a public health professional and advocate spans over 15 years, with roles in health research, prenatal health education, and mental health counseling. She currently serves as an Executive Board Member for the Divine Grace Foundation, Nutrition Security Solutions, and United Black Mothers of America.

Prior to becoming a physician, Dr. Pierre received certifications in prenatal and Kundalini yoga, which she emphatically integrates into her patient care protocols.

Her love of patient care has expanded into global health initiatives, participating in medical missions in Haiti, Mexico, and Kenya. Preceding the explosion of the "natural hair movement", Dr. Pierre was an influencer whose tips for healthy hair growth, treatment and styling were widely sought after in the natural hair community. When she is not seeing patients, Dr. Pierre enjoys prayer and meditation, traveling, fashion, reading, and cooking vegetarian meals that make meat lovers reconsider.

Find Dr. Pierre online at:

https://www.drjpierre.com/

"

*Change will not come if we wait
for some other person or some other
time. We are the ones we've been
waiting for. We are the change
that we seek.*

– Barack Obama

"

Continuing the Family Legacy While Breaking Stereotypes

by Azra Khalfan-Kermali

You've heard the African Proverb, "it takes a village"? When it comes to my success and failures, I always thank God for all the bounties around me. In my entrepreneurial journey, I have gained insight from clients, organizations, friends, mentors, advisors, and even my suppliers. Even in my mistakes or misfortunes, I can get back up and continue. My parents were a huge influence and impact on my life. They gave me all the best life can offer and empowered me to make my own decisions. Because of that, I pray and wish that I can do the same for others. I always hope that this business will be passed on to a member of our family, and I have hope my granddaughter will one day carry on the torch and lead this company.

When I first started, one of the major challenges I was faced with was the culture around how the abilities of women were doubted. Just to clarify, these cultures have nothing to do with religious values, because if anything, my faith (Islam) is designed to treat women with so much justice accordingly. And, the Prophet Muhammad (peace and blessings upon him and his family), was married to a successful businesswoman, Sayedana Khatija bint Khuwalid who is one of the best role models when it comes to social entrepreneurship.

Initially, I thought it was the culture our family tried so much to hold on to after moving to the west. I cannot stop thanking God for giving me a visionary father who honors and respects women. To recognize him for naming the business after me despite having an elder son is just a drop in a vast ocean. The underlying foundation he built was dynamic and empowering. The company, *Plaques by Azra*, was a gift to my mom. She was always at the forefront. But even in his discussions, it was clear, my father is a man who was way ahead of his time; someone who has a love for humanity, despite their race, gender, religion, ethnic background, or socio-economic status.

Unfortunately, there were times where I heard misogynistic noises from others around me. It was obvious that some of these men had a sense of entitlement over women, that they lacked confidence, and started to project negativity my way. Some would imply that my religious covering would interfere in closing deals or maybe result in losing clients. Despite having the ability to shut down some of the noises, it was subconsciously holding me back from attending important meetings in person when I first joined the company.

Ironically, the people who they imagined would discriminate against me the most, were the ones who taught me that my dressing was a symbol of strength, a commitment to my beliefs, and the ability to be true to who I am. They saw it as a matter of principle and transparency; to uphold my values and bring these positive attributes to the table. I have been told many times that I blazed the trail for younger girls and other women. That I stood up for what I wanted and this has made it easier for them. An example that comes to mind is at an NMSDC National Conference when a lady in her late 50's or early 60's came up to me and asked for a photograph together. Afterward, she explained that she wanted the photo to show her son. He always would ask her to remove her head covering before attending a conference. She said after hearing my speech on stage that day, she found the courage to dress the way she wanted in the future. She would no longer agree to conform or compromise for trying to fit in the corporate world. During other similar panel discussions, I would also share my positive experiences on gaining access to prayer space at business events with some of the men who were struggling at their professional workspaces. I hope that I can educate and encourage as many as people to learn that we must all do our best to live in harmony and be true to ourselves. When it comes to gender equality or freedom to practice religion, we must work diligently so that others are no longer able to impose implicit biases. The best way to improve in these areas to find justice is to keep men as part of the equation and to have courageous conversations with dialogues.

In recent years, I have had the honor to attend two summits hosted by the Tory Burch Foundation. The content made me understand that we are all responsible to educate and embrace one another. What I realized is that biases are biases; they can be around women, or around black people, or anyone who doesn't have an upper hand. During the murder of George Floyd, I was deeply hurt because I started to look inwards and question my contribution towards standing against this type of injustice. It made me realize, I have still so much to learn. There is so much work I need to do to fulfill my purpose. That is what motivates me, the desire to do whatever I can so that my Lord is pleased with me. While attending these summits helped me unveil some of the layers around a verse that is one of my favorites. *"In the name of Allah, Most Gracious, Most Merciful. O mankind! We created you from a single (pair) of a male and a female, and made you into nations and tribes, that ye may know each other (not that ye may despise (each other). Verily the most honored of you in the sight of Allah is (he who is) the most righteous of you. And Allah has full knowledge and is well acquainted (with all things)." Holy Qur'an Chapter 49, verse 13.*

I remember coming home from the first summit and realizing that I just spent the entire day learning about the depth of just this one verse. And I still had loads to learn. Our life has a purpose greater than just the mundane; we must continue to learn about discrimination and implicit biases and then help disperse that information.

The framework of our business was pretty much laid out for me by my parents, and by watching them I learned most of the fundamental values, it was clear I adored them and wanted to follow in their footsteps.

Growing up, our small business was an integral part of our lives. When I was young, my parents bestowed on me the responsibility of counting and packing. After school activities included learning new accounting software that they were transitioning to. Whilst spending time on homework, I subconsciously was picking up on how my parents were balancing between raising a family, running a family business, and selflessly serving the extended family and community. They were always very content and our home was always a place where family crashed over the weekend from near and far. Many would come to seek advice on business and life in general. During the holidays, we would travel all over the USA to faith-based conferences where our company would have a booth to display all the products they created for a sub-division. This division became the largest Muslim Award Company in the world; catering mostly to Centers and Schools serving the Muslim Community in the west.

Our core business is in the industry of manufacturing awards, signs, and decals. We are more of a boutique type of service. Many of our awards have been presented to global leaders, government officials, and men, women, and children who have gone above and beyond. Due to COVID19, our business came to a screeching halt, we pivoted to providing our customers with PPE including floor vinyl, temporary signage, and face shields. The pandemic has made everything change and thanks to my advisor, I realized we had to take the leap and pivot again. That meant pivoting myself and my business, working extra hours, and implementing new technology and ideas. But I am optimistic. It is very exciting to explore new ideas. I realize that I may not have overnight success, but I am content with what I have and feel grounded. My reasons to set new goals and pivot are because of the current pandemic. This time I am keen on embedding some of my passions into the new business plan's DNA.

I am a firm believer that it is very important to live a life that encompasses all the aspects that are fulfilling. When I first joined the company, my goals were focused on building wealth and continuing our family legacy. I was fortunate to quickly realize the importance of balancing work/spirituality/life. Wealth would only take care of my material needs. To live a fulfilled life, my focus had to involve investing in the things I loved and believed in and feeding my soul. Once the inner being is satisfied, the workflows very well. My soul is fueled by engaging in conversations that help me grow spiritually. For years I actively engaged in interfaith events and recently through monthly interfaith dialogue circles with people from other backgrounds and beliefs. This connection with others awakens my spirit and affirms my faith further. It is also incredible how close we become like sisters.

Our community and family are also an incredible source of strength for me. Although being away from those whom I love can be very challenging. My husband Kazim and I spent many years apart, but we would travel together often to make up for the lost time. Travel also fuels my soul and I enjoy learning about other cultures, religions, and food. I have had the privilege to volunteer in war-torn or underprivileged nations. Serving and living with people who have limited resources allows me to be grateful for every little blessing I have. In my life, I have lived in, New York City, Dar es Salaam, and Dubai. I enjoy exploring locally whenever I can if I am not traveling.

The pandemic has forced many of us to restructure, reevaluate and rewind. Over the years, I have learned (and need to learn over again), that I must surrender and graciously accept that ultimately God has control over everything. During the years, my mom always guided me in this area. If my efforts and investment of time are not met with results, it doesn't equate to being a failure; I must continue to persist. During the time I worked with her, if she ever saw that I was anxious or overly worried about winning a contract or large project, she would calmly explain that I should just take a step back and leave it in the hands of God. She advised that I should continue to make all the efforts and put in the hard work, but ultimately believe that I will only receive what is meant to come my way.

At the beginning of the pandemic, I relied on my savings. After a few months, I received some loans and grants. That is keeping me afloat. I am heavily marketing at the moment and was very fortunate to have received an opportunity to exhibit at a national conference through corporate sponsorship. I am struggling to pay rent and to find a new place to move to if I am forced to. We have been at our location for over 35 years and it is one of the most difficult moves I have had to consider.

In the past, our family took advantage of loans and leases on equipment, and it made a lot of sense to do so. My mom was very prudent and made the right investments. When I took over the company I was shy to take loans and bootstrapped most of the way. I would utilize credit cards and always make sure I was not in debt. When Hurricane Sandy hit, I applied for a loan which also led me to take a microloan. It was the best move I could ever make.

Of course, there are many lessons I have come to realize as I mature and face the next decade of my life. I wish I didn't micromanage as much. I realized that I should invest in hiring a team of experts to grow my business, I would have been way ahead. My husband has encouraged this to me before as well. I was fortunate to shadow him running his business in Tanzania and we would spend hours discussing our family businesses. He is a savvy, successful, and serious businessman to say the least. But he always encourages me to put my parents and son first. We were always in sync about me learning new things and setting higher goals. Right now, I am forcing myself to pivot into an area I was shy in. The more I take steps toward the new venture, the easier it is getting. I would advise all women to step outside of their comfort zone and take risks. It's never too late, and you are a work in progress.

During recent years, I have come to understand the high level of risks that entrepreneurs take. Anyone who has a 9-5 job, knows that at the end of the week, they will go home with a paycheck. It works very differently for entrepreneurs. You may go months without pay. You prioritize individuals and relationship building. You take into account expenses before you factor in yourself. You take risks because you believe in what you do. This isn't the best practice, but those were the risks I took because I love my family and believe in what we do.

Finally, I have found a way to thoroughly enjoy my work over the years. During seasonal peaks, it brings me so much joy serving my customers. There are many that I found myself making lasting relationships. Some continue to share how our products and services helped them with getting results; that is so satisfying. Whether it is for a school, a business, or a non-profit, people love getting recognition through awards. Over the years, I have had some clients that my parents worked with, and I get to carry on that responsibility.

There is no doubt that I weathered many storms and when I was faced with problems in my personal life, it would throw me off the track a little. That is what makes me human. I remember clearly a textbook I received in 2nd Grade. The title was "Never Give Up". Whenever I was able to push through the hard times, or when my hard work has paid off, that title comes to mind, reminding me that I must persist and have patience. My life is far from a bed of roses, but I try to make a beautiful garden with what I have and continue to pray for whatever is best.

My greatest teachers have been my parents, mentors, and advisors. As for all my supporters, mentors, and advisors, my prayers remain for them, and may they reap the reward as I strive to pay it forward.

It is an honor and privilege to serve my parents and continue their legacy. I can't help myself to dream far and big. It makes me think of my mom, how it all started when she was in her teens, shadowing her elder brothers in their family business somewhere in the rural part of Tanzania before she met my father, who also in his teens, discovered his talent as a commercial artist. A man who was ambitious and gained a degree through a correspondence course while living in Tanzania. A man who sacrificed so much in his early years for the sake of his family and found fulfillment in publishing the Qur'an in the USA years later. The two of them, united and committed to building a better future. Fifty years later, their daughter is sharing their story to hopefully inspire others. They dared to dream big and so will I! Will you?

About Azra Khalfan-Kermali

Azra Khalfan-Kermali is the CEO of Plaques by Azra and Signs and Lucite Products. Born and raised in Queens, New York, at the age of 18, she moved to her husband's and parent's hometown in Tanzania for 6 years.

Living in a third-world country and becoming a mother completely changed her perspective in life. Upon her return to the USA, she pursued her education in Business, first at the Queens Borough Community College, and then at the College of Old Westbury. She has been managing her family's businesses for over 20 years.

Azra has been involved with community fundraising (Comfort Aid International) and awareness towards assisting orphans, widows, empowerment through education, and the building of wells. She served on the Board of TPNY, a non for profit organization advocating for victims of Domestic Violence.

Azra lives in New York and Dubai with her husband Kazim, her parents, and her son Muhammadali.

Find Azra online at:

http://www.azra.com/about/

"

*Be passionate and move forward
with gusto every single hour of every
single day until you reach your goal.*

-Ava Duvernay

Making Healthcare Accessible

by Dr. Shelley Cooper

My name is Dr. Shelley Cooper and I am the CEO and Founder of Diversity Telehealth. I am a telehealth specialist where I consult and design telehealth solutions for medical facilities such as federally qualified health centers, schools, and hospitals. When organizations are in search of ways to increase access to healthcare for their patients, they contact Diversity Telehealth. There are several ways I provide telehealth for organizations, communities, and individuals.

Ever since I was a young girl, I always enjoyed making things and earning extra money. In middle school, I would knit small coin purses and sell them. I got my first job as a cashier at a local hamburger chain when I was 15 years old. At that time, we were required to be 16 years old to work outside the home. I lied to get the job but forgot about the lie and came in to work on my 16th birthday ready to celebrate my newfound freedom. During college, I sold Mary Kay Cosmetics, Avon, Tupperware, Amway, and any other types of products that allowed me to earn income. College was paid for with savings from summer jobs, scholarships, grants, and loans. I sewed hems into my friends' jeans, typed term papers, and several other side hustles as I earned a bachelor's degree in business administration from the University of Missouri at Columbia in 1983.

Upon graduation, I began working as an Officer Trainee at my Inroads sponsoring company, Commerce Bank of Kansas City. Later, my high school sweetheart and I married in 1985 and I moved on to work for Sprint where I held a variety of accounting, human resources, and telecommunications positions. Following the birth of my two daughters, I left the corporate world and started Cooper Business Services, a resume writing, and desktop publishing business. I compiled my experience and knowledge in human resources into writing the "Job Finding Kit", a job search workbook and guide for drafting resumes and cover letters for job seekers. It sold a few copies and helped me gain several clients. Next, I was hired as an Assistant Teacher at a Montessori School while I earned a Business Teacher license. When I completed my courses and passed the teacher's exams, I began teaching 3rd grade at a small Catholic school. Two years later, I moved on to teach Computer Applications and Career Explorations at a middle school in my neighborhood. Teaching at the middle school allowed me to work in the same district where my daughters attended school. That way I could be more involved in their activities and attend their class events. Soon thereafter, I earned a Master of Arts in Teaching which required several evening courses and extra projects. It was hard to work all day, take care of the housework, care for the kids and spend time with my husband, but I knew a higher-level degree would bring more money and improve my career potential.

When my daughters were beginning 4th and 6th grades, an opportunity to earn scholarships at the local neighborhood private school became available. It was a lottery system and required that we make a commitment to pay a portion of the tuition in order to qualify. When we were accepted, we moved them to the local Catholic school and my son was born a little while later. Even though the school was a large financial commitment, it provided a better environment for my kids. When the school needed a computer teacher, I was offered the job and I taught at the same Catholic school my kids attended for 15 years. Then they were able to attend private school - tuition-free. What a blessing! Throughout my years of working in education, I made intermittent attempts at entrepreneurship to make ends meet. I started a tutoring service, operated a desktop publishing and business consulting while working full time at each of the schools. During my final years of teaching, I began to work on my doctoral degree in Instructional Technology and Distance Education. Also, while teaching full-time and pursuing my doctoral degree, I taught at a local state university. My doctoral rotations led to several areas of focus where one could provide services from a distance using technology: law, education, and finally medicine. That is where I thought I could provide the most benefit to my community.

I completed my telemedicine training at the University of Arizona and telehealth mentoring at the University of Kansas. I earned my Doctor of Education (Instructional Technology & Distance Education) degree at Nova Southeastern University. My dissertation, "Opinion Leaders' Perspective of the Benefits and Barriers in Telemedicine: A Grounded Theory Study of Telehealth in the Midwest," was an in-depth exploration of the legal, legislative, ethical, financial, and equipment issues related to telemedicine.

I'd planned to continue teaching after I completed my doctorate but, my field of study was telemedicine and it was difficult to put my newly discovered skills into practice as I continued working at the school. So, I decided to put my degree to work. In 2015, I founded Diversity Telehealth, LLC in Kansas City, Missouri. I filed articles of incorporation with the state, ordered business cards, rented office space, and began looking for customers. Most people had never heard of telemedicine/ telehealth, so I needed to educate them on the features and benefits of telehealth. That was five years ago. I've been in the field of telemedicine ever since. Diversity Telehealth brings healthcare to all communities, especially underserved populations by collaborating with federally qualified health centers, schools, and community organizations. My company is located in the Historic 18th & Vine Jazz District and promotes virtual health care and behavioral therapy services remotely to schools, businesses, and underserved communities.

When the school budget was strained, I agreed to work 4 days a week and use one day for promoting my telehealth business. It was very difficult to meet with clients, take business calls and work on my business while teaching four days a week but, I wanted to stay at the school where my children had grown up in and I had so many friends and positive parent relationships. However, I believe God had another plan for me.

Everything came to a head a few months after school resumed. There was a parent who made several derogatory remarks to me during our fall Parent Conferences. His comments were so hurtful and demeaning that I called my principal in to intervene. He continued to degrade me and there wasn't much said in my defense. I'd had differences in opinion with parents in the past, but this situation was personal and directly aimed at my character and qualifications. I had been the only African American teacher in the school's 90-year history. It never occurred to me that one of the parents could dislike me for that reason. Naïve, I know, but things had always gone well, and I thought we were "past" that type of narrow-minded thinking. But on that day, I felt deep in my spirit that my time at the school had come to an end and that I should move on to do what I had been training to do. I no longer felt that I belonged there or that I was appreciated for what I could contribute to the environment. Incident after the incident occurred that left me feeling that the school was no longer my home. I continued to put forth the effort but, those events stung me in a way I hadn't anticipated. The final blow was my annual evaluation. I'd normally received "Meets Expectations" and a few "Exceeds Expectations" during my annual reviews. That wasn't to be the case this time. As a matter of fact, my principal, with whom I felt I had a strong and close relationship, presented me with an evaluation where she said I "Did Not Meet Expectations" in 8 areas! Never before had such a thing happened! I was shocked and hurt, to say the least. Why hadn't these areas of dissatisfaction been brought to me over the course of the school year? There were so many areas of unmet expectations that it seemed like a dream or more likely a nightmare. I was able to negotiate 5 of the bad marks off of the review, but 3 remained. Three more than I'd ever received in my lifetime. Was this the school's way of showing me the door or was it a result of the influence of the negative event with the parent or were there signs present that I'd been ignoring my entire final year in teaching? At any rate, I believed it was time for me to move on. Twenty-five years in education seemed like a great ending for me. It was time to transition into what I had been training to do, telemedicine. The delivery of healthcare and health-related education from a distance, using technology.

I tried several times to work with local medical clinics. Finally, a group of federally qualified health centers in St. Louis needed someone to help them with telehealth training. I collaborated with CareSTL formerly Myrtle Hilliard Davis Comprehensive Health Center (MHDCHC) to assess its telemedicine needs, train the staff and coordinate the implementation of telehealth programming. I created the telehealth infrastructure to allow CareSTL to begin offering telemedicine services to its patients. As a result, the center is equipped to offer telehealth services to Hazelwood and Riverview Gardens school districts. Currently, CareSTL is the pilot organization entrusted to train students at St. Louis University on using telehealth to care for vulnerable populations with limited resources. Mrs. Angela Clabon, CEO of CareSTL provided the following testimonial. "Diversity Telehealth made a huge impact! Our partnership with Diversity Telehealth empowered us to seek new opportunities to provide care to more people through school-based health centers. Thanks for everything, Dr. Cooper. If you hadn't enlightened me to the benefits of telehealth, the center would be still struggling with expanding access to our youth during the school season."

When I'd completed the project for CareSTL, I was able to use that experience to prove to other clinics that I had the skill set to design their solutions. Swope Health Services retained me to assist them with their telepsychiatry offering and guidance toward future telehealth programming endeavors. I concentrated on providing telehealth consulting with Federally Qualified Health Centers because it serves underserved communities. "Diversity Telehealth provided research and advice to Swope Health Services as they approached the expansion of their telehealth initiatives" stated Mark Miller, Vice President of Behavioral Health at Swope Health Services.

The work with those two organizations allowed me to gain exposure to more medical locations. In the meantime, I attended multiple telemedicine conferences where I presented my doctoral research, reserved booth space in the exhibit hall, attended events hosted by the local Chamber of Commerce, registered my company as a Women-owned, Minority-owned, and disadvantaged company. I also presented my research at conferences and maintain memberships at the following associations: American Telemedicine Association (ATA), Health Information Management System Society (HIMSS), School-based Health Alliance (SBHA), United States Distance Learning Association (USDLA), and Missouri Telehealth Network (MTN). These conferences allowed me to have exposure to subject matter experts and expand my professional network.

Other promotional activities included attending multiple networking events where I passed out hundreds of business cards. I held drawings at business events where I could collect email addresses of potential clients. I joined a local small business networking group. The Kauffman Foundation offered a few training sessions for entrepreneurs called Kauffman Fast Track and Kauffman Tech Track where business essentials were taught and guest speakers shared information about their companies. I worked with a SCORE volunteer and attended training sessions at the Community Colleges in my area. The Better Business Bureau invited me to become a member and offered numerous resources. The Chamber of Commerce and nearby community college offered Minority Development Procurement gatherings where decision-makers were available to learn about small businesses. I had brochures made and mailed them to potential clients. Social media outlets were helpful for informing connections of achievements earned by Diversity Telehealth, for example, LinkedIn, Facebook, and Twitter.

In 2017, I designed and implemented an eight-week Pediatric Telebehavioral Health (PTBH) pilot program at Benjamin Banneker Charter Academy that allowed children in kindergarten through fourth grade to meet weekly with a behavioral health therapist using their laptops. I designed and coordinated the scheduling among the staff, students, and providers. FreeState Healthcare (Wichita, KS) provided in-kind software support and Humana donated a stipend for the provider. "It was evident the services provided during the brief sessions rendered a notable change in each student's behavior." – Dr. Marian Brown, Superintendent, Benjamin Banneker Charter Academy.

In 2018, Diversity Telehealth partnered with the University of Missouri School of Medicine-Asthma Ready Communities on its Teaming Up for Asthma Control initiative within the Kansas City, Missouri School District. This project is aligned with patient-centered education, care, and population health for an underserved minority community in Kansas City. In addition, I have been involved in implementing the first school-based asthma telehealth pilot in Kansas City. I am also assisting in generating provider and strategic partnerships within the community. In addition, Diversity Telehealth has been selected as a partner with the Kansas City, Missouri School District.

As a result of my work with Asthma Ready Communities, one of its major contributors requested that I collaborate with her company in supervising the study involving adolescent children. REESSI, Research, Evaluation & Social Solutions, Inc's president Dr. Laverne Morrow Carter retained me to serve as a consulting Study Director on a pilot project to develop a psychosocial serious learning game for adolescents living in under-resourced families and communities.

Due to the large number of underserved individuals who could not afford telehealth service, I created a philanthropic arm for her company called Diversity Telehealth Community Network, Inc. 501c3. I raise money through Facebook fundraisers, and I make personal donations in order to provide free Teladoc memberships to families in need at True Light Family Resource Center and Hope Faith Ministries.

Healthcare is needed by all people, regardless of race, sexual orientation, religion, etc. In order to help make this possible, Rashaan Gilmore, CEO of BlaqOut, is collaborating with Diversity Telehealth to create telehealth solutions that assist HIV populations to gain confidential and culturally competent access to healthcare. Currently, Diversity Telehealth is providing access to virtual healthcare to several of its members. BlaqOut is a united community of individual advocates, community activists, and healthcare professionals who work to address the psychosocial and environmental challenges faced by Black MSM in the Greater Kansas City Area. We plan to expand the availability of services as funding allows.

Diversity Telehealth is also seeking to provide the opportunity of virtual healthcare to Spanish-speaking patients who may find it difficult to leave work to see a doctor. I have been working with Index Lingua, a Kansas City-based translation service, to design a Spanish website called Doctor Por Telefono. Clients can visit www.doctorportelefono.com to register for medical services provided by Spanish-speaking doctors through an app on their phone or computer. These services were spotlighted at the Shawnee Mission Kansas School District's Migrant Education Program Family Enrichment Event where Spanish-speaking families were able to register for telehealth services.

In 2018, my father died unexpectedly in his sleep. He had 2 chronic diseases and saw his doctor regularly. He had a doctor's appointment scheduled to take place just a few days after he passed away...he never made it.

Afterward, I began to wonder, "What if we could have gotten him into his doctor sooner?" At the time, I was helping medical clinics design their telehealth solutions and one of their biggest problems was high no-show rates. Around 25% or 1 in 4 medical appointments end up as no-shows or late cancellations and that equals billions of dollars in lost revenue each year.

That's why I founded SureShow, a revenue-generating platform that replaces no-show medical appointments with billable telehealth visits. I realized I could create a solution that fills downtime with on-demand telehealth visits. More people will see their doctors when they need to. With SureShow, everybody wins. Patients get more care and doctors get paid for lost time.

I knew this would have the greatest impact on the most medically fragile patients, like my father, who make up about 50% of the U.S. population.

We've designed SureShow to be easy and secure for both providers and patients to use. And, importantly, it's interoperable with all major electronic health records, so it works seamlessly with Epic, Cerner, and other software platforms.

Here's how it works. Doctors identify patients in need of additional care and move them into our SureShow queue. When there's a no-show, SureShow notifies patients in the queue that an appointment is available. Once they accept the invitation, the patient is connected to the doctor for a telehealth visit. It's that simple! Beyond ease of use, we've designed the platform to encourage rapid adoption: Interoperability with all major electronic health records creates seamless integration, while HIPAA Compliance and high levels of security ensure practitioner confidence that all data is secure. And we are the first to provide this solution with our patent-pending technology.

Beyond our initial target of medical clinics, our platform can be extended to any industry where no-shows can be handled by conference call or video visit. Although major Electronic Medical Record providers such as Epic have telehealth capabilities, there is no solution available that provides a way to replace no-shows with billable telehealth visits. SureShow's automated scheduling feature is a revolutionary way of compiling patients in the wait-listed queue that increases the likelihood of successfully filling the no-show slots.

Since our launch at the beginning of 2020, we've been in conversations with 30 potential clients with whom we've performed 25 demonstrations and have now secured 3 Letters of Intent. In addition, we've landed a contract with a key channel partner that services over 21,000 facilities nationwide. In mid-October 2020, we began a trial pilot program with a small private medical practice where we are working out any possible glitches and collecting customer information on how to make SureShow a better product when it is offered to additional clinics. Larger medical facilities are starting to take notice.

Our team consists of myself and our Chief Technology Officer who is medically trained as well as a software developer, with years of experience at Cerner and a large hospital system.

Our advisors bring expertise in scaling early-stage tech startups and healthcare sales strategies. Together, we are the perfect team to make SureShow a successful and profitable organization.

There has never been a better time to introduce a solution like SureShow. We're at a tipping point with telehealth. Adoption is at its highest and at the same time, it has become even more challenging for medically fragile patients to go to the doctor. This means 2 things: telehealth is going to become more critical for people who need healthcare. And it has become even easier for insurance companies to reimburse telehealth visits. So SureShow is perfectly positioned as telehealth becomes more commonplace. I hope this option is used on a widespread basis. And hopefully, no more daughters should have to share a similar story.

My personal/family life

I am a wife, mother, and grandmother. We live in the same modest home that we moved into when we were married in 1985. My husband and I have been married for 35 years. All of our children were born into and moved out of this home. I have 3 grown children, daughter Sydney, 32; daughter 30 Danielle and son Brandon, Jr. 20. We also have 3 grand-children: Janelle, 7, Jaylen 4, and Olivia 3. At one time, my husband was a science teacher and Assistant Pastor of our local Missionary Baptist Church, but now enjoys genealogical projects and working in his garden.

Managing work/life balance

I seem to be in an "All or Nothing" gear right now. Since my kids are grown and my husband and I are free to explore our own interests, I have been putting more of my energies into Diversity Telehealth and SureShow. Sometimes I find myself working into the late-night hours, getting very little sleep, and getting up early to work on projects. This probably isn't the best example of work/life balance. However, I added an elliptical machine to my office and my goal is to get more exercise instead of working at my desk for hours on end. I am adding healthier options to my diet and drinking more water. I don't plan to replace my evening cocktail. (smile)

Mindset while on one's pathway to Rise

The mindset needed to be on the pathway to Rise is one of tenacity and backup plans. During one of my earlier pitch presentations, I discovered that the software on my laptop was outdated and wasn't working well with the software needed to deliver my pitch to a national audience. As a result, I wasn't able to share my pitch with potential investors and missed out on competing for $10,000! I was embarrassed and disappointed in myself that I didn't have a back-up plan, a Plan B for emergencies. That was a very strong lesson learned. Always have a Plan B ready and waiting, just in case things go wrong. The same thing happened during the Her Rise Conference. I was one of five finalists to deliver my pitch. We'd practiced the line-up a few days ahead and things were going great. I was the last presenter and had my slides ready to present to the virtual audience. When my name was called and I tried to share my slides, I continued to receive error messages. Since that had happened just a few days prior, I had a backup plan. I had my pitch on note cards and didn't use the slides. I didn't think it went as well as a discussion but I won First Place!

A similar thing took place two days later. I was delivering my pitch, live in front of over 100 investors. I was the eighth out of eight presenters. I'd memorized my pitch because no one was using note cards and there were no slides or props allowed. I had practiced for weeks and felt confident that I could deliver my presentation. I was wearing my favorite dress; the one I wore when I met and took pictures with Daymond John. My name was called and my entry music Alicia Keys' song, _Girl on Fire_ was playing. I walked onto the stage and began the pitch I'd practiced a hundred times in front of the mirror, my husband, my dogs, and any of my friends who made the mistake of calling me. It started out smoothly, and then I made the mistake of making eye contact with a member of the audience for a little too long and I COMPLETELY FORGOT EVERYTHING I WAS SUPPOSED TO SAY! I closed my eyes and tried to visualize the order of the paragraphs, Nothing! When I opened my eyes, I was staring into the bright lights and froze with fear (on the inside) but, on the outside, I kept walking on the stage and said something like, "It's a lot harder to stand up here than it looks". The audience responded with encouraging rounds of applause and I was able to get through the rest of the pitch. Some of the words were out of order, some were left out altogether. But I stayed on the stage and finished my pitch. I thought I'd blown the whole thing. I was ready to take my purse and go home until the master of ceremonies began to announce the investors' decision on who was to receive funding. I was the overall winner! I won over $25,500! My lesson during that experience was to keep going, even when it looks like you've messed things up so badly that you just want to sneak out the back door. Just give it your best, pray and move on.

Funding my business

I funded my business with credit cards, savings, and consulting assignments. I worked temporary jobs as a receptionist, visiting professor at a charter school, and other side hustles. While accepting jobs that took me away from my main focus, I always talked about my business and handed out business cards everywhere I went (unless it was against the company's policy). It was similar to showing off pictures of my kids or dogs or any other object of pride.

Skills I developed as an employee

While working for various companies throughout my lifetime, I've always tried to do my best. That's what I've told my kids and students, "Do your best work". Sometimes it's difficult to do my best work when I look around and it seems like others are "half-stepping" or barely trying but receive accolades and praise for a bad performance. It is unfair and makes me angry and discouraged. However, I have to try to overlook them and do my personal best. There will always be unfair situations, I'm working on trying to ignore those circumstances and push forward to concentrate on what I've been put on this earth to do.

Goals for my business and career

My goals for Diversity Telehealth have always been to bring healthcare into underserved areas using technology. SureShow is an example of how I'm continuing to strive toward that goal.

Exit strategy for leaving a job

When I left my job, I left on good and professional terms. Even though I felt my evaluation was unfair and there were situations that should have been handled differently, I did not react in an unprofessional manner. I think it's important to remember that there are so many connections between previous employers, colleagues, and potential clients that you should leave on the best possible footing. Whenever I see people from previous work environments, I try to remember the good times or concentrate on the happy memories of our time together. If I can't do that, I talk about the weather. It's a safe topic.

Sustaining my business

Currently, Diversity Telehealth is gaining traction in the telehealth space. When the COVID-19 pandemic took over the planet, most people began to shelter in place. They weren't able to have traditional face-to-face medical appointments and telehealth became the next best thing. As a result, Diversity Telehealth and my SureShow app have gained more attention. I have been reaching out to more companies about potential telehealth solutions and investors have begun to contact me about investing in SureShow. The future looks bright.

Hiring and outsourcing staff

I do not have any full-time, permanent employees. However, when I have a project that requires additional skills, I enter into a contract with specialists who can meet those needs. For example, my doctor por Telefono website is in Spanish. I pay a college student to make updates and revisions to the site. She also performs some of the administrative tasks that need to be done but I don't have time to do it. Outsourcing some of the other tasks or collaborating with colleagues has become a great way to expand my customer base without hiring additional staff.

Risks and sacrifices in growing my business

There have been situations when people have approached me with an opportunity to work for them and it's not a good fit for me. It might seem like a good idea in the beginning, but after doing my research, I discover there isn't much substance to the proposal. When an offer is presented to me, I like to have it checked out by my attorney and do as much online research as possible. My method of decision making has been, "When in doubt, don't". This process has served me well in the past.

Additional resources that have helped you start or grow your business.

There are many online resources for starting and growing a business. Many of the software platforms offer a free version that can be used on a small scale. HubSpot is a perfect example. It offers a wealth of tools to help get organized. Google also has many free tools that can be helpful in running a business. If you set up a Gmail account for registering for webinars and workshops, the resulting sales emails will not flood your primary email account. Social media is a free (cost, not time) way to present your business to your local and national marketplace. Associations have free events and offer opportunities to network with colleagues and potential clients. YouTube has been a good way to learn about new software and processes for conducting business. Sometimes your competitors are a good way to see what's being offered. Shopping the competition and visiting their social media outlets can give you ideas on what's going on in the marketplace. Depending on your product and customer base, Facebook and LinkedIn can be nice ways to connect to potential clients/customers and to sell your products/services.

About Dr. Shelley Cooper

Dr. Shelley J Cooper founded Diversity Telehealth in 2015, a telemedicine consulting firm that specializes in bringing healthcare to underserved populations in diverse communities.

Career highlights include:

- 25 years education experience (PreK – HigherEd)
- Doctorate in Instructional Technology & Distance Education
- Dissertation: Telemedicine Adoption
- Telemedicine Training: University of Arizona (Telemedicine)
- Telemedicine Job Shadow – University of Kansas (Telemedicine)
- Master's Arts in Teaching
- Bachelor's Degree in Business

Find Dr. Cooper online at:

linkedin.com/in/dr-shelley-cooper-06a4662/

"

I learned early on the magic of life is having a vison, having faith and then going for it.

– Elaine Welteroth

"

4SYT Industries

by Sheena Parker

How it started-How it's going

My SHEpreneur story starts from the age of 12 when I needed money. Not just candy and toy money but clothes, grocery, and bus fare money. We were POOR poor. Not just, "My momma worked 2 jobs poor.", but my momma worked NO job poorly. But everyone else was poor too- so this was life. Some people say hustlers can be made; my belief is, they are BORN THIS WAY. Whether the "hustle spirit" shows itself later rather than sooner, or not; there's a special something that shows up in a person when they have their balls to the wall!

That 1st Hustler's Call came to me when I drew signs on a piece of notebook paper to hang up around my apartment building, trying to sell my basketball and baseball cards. \

One thing my mother did, she ensured the 5 of us received toys for Christmas from every donated source possible. So I always "requested" trading cards and electronics. At first, the cards were a hobby, then they became merchandise. Along with my pogs & slammers, 1-3 of my 4 walkmans, and duplicate board games. Only #80sBabies can relate.

My ideation of hustling or earning extra cash came from watching tv. Growing up, I didn't know a single business owner - I didn't even understand the concept of what business was. There were about 3-4 people in my family who had a job; so the abundance of money was always a foreign concept to me. We were fine as long as some sort of income came in on the 1st of the month.

I started my first W2 job at a nun's retirement home at 14 using my school ID; then using that same ID to open my 1st bank account. No guidance, no direction, just an inquisitive mind. Since that 1st job, I've had *many* jobs (over 30); sometimes 2 or 3 at the same time. MANY businesses, side hustles, and HUSTLE-hustles along the way. Everything from selling knives to working at a laundromat, to waitressing, block-buster, circuit city, to credit repair, to hustling oils, owning a massage studio, to website creation, to uber....before it was uber; YOU NAME IT!

I've been fortunate enough to continue to serve in the US Army for over 18 years; serving as a Signal Warrant Officer in the Information Technology space (fancy title for IT Manager). Being in the military, especially in my field, with my rank, is like a unicorn riding on the back of Pegasas. Some people would tell you, being in the military can be a gift and a curse. Why a curse? Anytime you are "trained" to think a certain way, you will develop a certain type of anxiety when things AREN'T that way. I have to remind myself, "Sheena, you slept on top of the mountains of Korea with no heat, no hot food, and dug a ditch to sh*t... business should be a BREEZE!" I use that as fuel for most of my decisions.

My jobs and businesses ran concurrently with the military when I was not on Active Duty. Many of them also were NOT Information Technology related. Throughout this time, I acquired a Bachelor's Degree in Business Administration with a concentration in Project Manage-ment. Having a business degree has always left a big question mark in my mind. Why get a degree for something you ABSOLUTELY do not need a degree for?! My degree was free - however, for others, I would advise using that same money to attend the School of Hard Knocks! In the trenches with your business, day in, and day out.

I have always had a passion for business and finance. Teaching budget classes, coupon classes, and dedicating many hours to ANYONE needing assistance with business startup, budget, or personal development!

Women are often underrepresented in many industries including the facility maintenance and construction industry. I am a Female Army Officer Veteran with a passion for helping women become unapologetically successful. Oftentimes, women struggle with being a mom, wife, employee, and businesswoman - all at the same time. We have outside forces demanding you choose one!

> *Tip: Be who you are and go for what YOU want. You cannot please others, including your family if you are not serving YOUR needs.* I am a seeker of knowledge in all things. I believe my drive for knowledge and teachings will be a benefit to those I am fortunate enough to connect with.

Six years ago, (2014), I tried out a long-time interest of mine - becoming a Real Estate Investor. My husband funded my 1st property - a condo. It was one of the worst investments I've ever made. However, with any failure comes many many lessons. Fast forward to 2016 and four properties later, I felt like being a landlord was NOT for me. I even started a Facebook trend called "Landlord Chronicles" - highlighting the woes of landlording bad tenants. Midway through landlording, I was led to acquisitions management and wholesaling. This is where **Sheena Investments** was born. I set it up as a Real Estate Investment Company. When that focus shifted to government contracting, I changed the business name to **4SYT Industries** *(pronounced for-site), a Real Estate & Facility Maintenance Company. "We make buildings beautiful again!"*

At this point in my life, I feel I've been in EVERY field. So it was only fitting for me to jump into completely uncharted territory; Government Contracting. In 2016, the conversation continued to come up in random interactions; so I decided to look into it. Fast forward to 2018, I bid on my 1st local contract, and won! WhooHoo! But then I learned I was significantly underbid, and could not find anyone to perform the job....so I had to cancel the acceptance of the award. This was an absolute blow to the ego. I tried again a month later on a different project, and won again! Yay!!! This one stuck, and it was over six figures - scary, exciting, and stressful all in one. My company provides Facility Maintenance Services to Federal, Local and Corporate Departments. These agencies have a regulatory spending goal to improve internal facilities or to provide services to the public. We bridge the gap between services and the government. Therefore, much of the work is done by specialty trade workers or General Contractors(GCs). We have to be VERY creative with time.

I wanted to stay connected to real estate so with the gift of government contracting, I was able to glide into the facility maintenance industry. Services include janitorial, floor repair, property management, real estate services, roof repair, painting, and more.

Work/Life WHAT?!

Within the wifepreneur, mompreneur, workpreneur, know that there really ISN'T such a thing as work/life balance. I am a wife to my wonderful husband who is also self-employed. He has always been so supportive of my crazy a** ideas! I am a mother to two teenage business owners in training (wishful thinking). My daughter recently launched her croc-charm business called **"Charmutopia"** on Etsy & Instagram. She is a WARRIOR! She balances school, volleyball, an actual job, and her new business at 15 - what more could I ask for!

I started 4SYT Industries while having a full-time job. I still hold this job as a matter of fact; due to my military obligation. If anything, running a business at this scale, has taught me the importance of time management and priorities. I'm up no later than 430am Monday - Sunday. I'm remote working most of the time so I have no choice but to get an early start to my day before the kids start "school" at home. In any given week, I have nephews and nieces over as well during school hours, my house can sound like a daycare!

Keeping this early morning time was definitely a challenge, as I've struggled since high school (20 years) to wake up early; and yes, it was also a struggle every single day in the military.

The only caution I have is knowing when to forgive yourself for focusing on other obligations. This is one of those secret locker room conversations that no one likes to talk about. Wanting to lock me in my home office to ignore my kids just so I can complete these last few invoices. Or telling my husband, we can't watch a movie tonight, because I have to submit this proposal by tomorrow! It's a very unpopular opinion.

Having my job income has definitely taken the pressure off of the need for high earnings; which can force you to make unreasonable choices in order to sustain your life. There are definitely pros and cons to this approach. I have had other businesses where no other income was coming in - this led to extreme stress and pressure on the business to perform. That is always an interesting topic to have. Should someone leave their job and step out on faith, or keep their job and only give their business a percentage of their attention. The truth is, I don't think it's a cut and dry answer; it literally depends. For me, I am obligated to my job. However, I was born an entrepreneur, that spirit cannot be smothered.

> *Tip: Before quitting your job, evaluate if your business can sustain your employee payroll? Can it fund your lifestyle? Are you getting rid of amazing job benefits? Will putting more time into your business make your business grow or only make you self-employed?*

Everyone's job is not as flexible as mine. There has to be a serious evaluation of your time and finances. Map out exactly what that looks like.

My original business goals have significantly changed from inception. Because I've had many businesses in the past, it was often challenging to discover what I wanted to do or ultimately accomplish. My vision and goals ALWAYS change, however, my overarching legacy goal remains the same - "To be a Matriarch and leave a viable system, product or idea for my family". With each life event, your goals can adjust. *Tip: I say, that's ok - as long as the end goal is clear.*

Many business owners of color often find it difficult to obtain funding for their business. This year, fortunately, and unfortunately, COVID helped my business with that. Thanks to wonderful organizations such as HerRise, The Doonie Fund, The Lift Fund, and The **Institute for Veterans and Military Families** (IVMF), 4SYT Industries was able to obtain grant funding that would not have otherwise been available!

In addition to that, 4SYT Industries was able to receive SBA funding. It goes without saying that 2020 has been (and continues to be) a year to remember - that's an understatement. Overall, however, lots of the feedback from the "field" is good feedback. Many of us have been forced out of our comfort zone - some of us are thriving more than ever. As for my business, my growth has skyrocketed, in many ways, due to COVID. 4SYT Industries offers janitorial services which meant entering into a market we had not intended to enter into! My business in itself IS sustainability - therefore, we are here as long as buildings are here! We have more emphasis on technology - which we should have been exploring in a better way from the beginning.

I know I am not typical, I am a young black woman in construction. Saying that is rare, is an understatement. Luckily that groomed me for what was to come in my business. I never have a problem walking into a room full of older white men who have been in construction for 20+ years. I am here to make my mark!

As always, being in business is a test of your faith, your feelings, your strength, your marriage, your level of parenthood, your friendships, and every other relationship! I have actually had friends removed from my life because I am so incredibly ambitious and laser-focused on growing my business and accomplishing my goals. That is very radical to those who do not have the same mindset. I had to accept that I AM radical - and everyone else has to deal with it. (Sorry-Not-Sorry). What appears to be sacrificed to others is just a part of the process for me. Going out and letting my hair down is not considered a break for me. Completing tasks are! When you do what you love, you do not need a break from it.

Motivation Keeps You Going When Things AREN'T Sexy

Everyone has thoughts of how their entrepreneurship journey should look. What your cute little logo will look like, what packages you're going to use, how you're going to pitch your family on your idea. Most of that.... are smoke and mirrors! Chances are, you're family won't support you, or even understand why you're doing what you're doing for that matter, you'll work more hours than you've ever worked in your life, you'll go broke funding this dream, and on top of all of that, something significant in your life will happen My motivation is **legacy**. This is absent in my family and many others' within our community. You have to have an insatiable drive to want AND achieve success. It can be a bloody match. So your vision has to be clear - with an uncertain path! I believe the outlook is everything. There were (and continue to be) many days I can only describe as pure depression. Other days, of disbelief, that such an achievement was happening for *me*. I have been scammed, personal finances attacked because of legal misguidance, the detriment to my home life - as many entrepreneurs have faced over and over again. Until you hear another entrepreneur's story, you think you are the only business owner silently - or publicly struggling. You must take every situation as a beautiful and painful lesson.

> *Tip: On days you feel down, IMMEDIATELY listen to something positive. Spiritual, uplifting music, YouTube motivational songs. Don't just sit there and take it - fight back!*

I have often been called a control freak within my life, my job, and my business! Control freaks have a hard time trusting anyone with their work. That quadruples when it comes to trusting someone with your baby, your business! The feeling is that no one will ever love your baby the way you will. And that is probably true. I had to be ok with that. I have hired and fired and made extremely irrational decisions based on the "feeling" that my "baby" was not being treated properly. However, we know that if your business cannot function without you, you have a hobby! That is the realist thing I've read all year. It is from the book "The E-Myth Revisited". My life goal is to have a functioning system so I can REALLY retire, learn to play the piano, learn three languages and visit my future house in Jamaica on the beach! The day-to-day grind reminds me of when you're growing a plant. You want to be a part of the entire process and you want to see the first sprout of green growth. However, once it's a large tree, it shouldn't need you nearly as much - if at all.

My ultimate goal is to not work 20 hours a day editing documents within my business. There's nothing fabulous about that! After a little self-check, I knew that the reason why I was not finding good people was that I was not clear about what I needed OR wanted! I realized that my hiring practices were completely off of emotion.

"Let me give that person a chance-they need help."

"That person is a veteran."

"They should already know how to do XYZ."

"Well if they don't know how to do the job, I can surely train them."

None of those things work with my lifestyle! So the decision was to figure out how much I would need to hire what I needed. At this time, I am happy to say that I do have a Capture Manager and Contract Manager Assistant. And they are the bomb! As this business grows and they learn their role more and more, I get closer and closer to the beach. I cannot fail to mention that paying for employees can be very scary!

Especially when your revenue is slim or nonexistent. One of my favorite books, "Run Like Clockwork", States that you should save or earn at least a 90 days salary for the employee or employees that you need. If you are unable to save that amount, you know that you cannot afford to pay them!

> **Tip: Try hiring someone part-time.**

"Success leaves clues." There is a tremendous amount of tenacity that goes along with being a successful member of society. Going along with the flow of life and not accomplishing anything is super easy! Most people reach the end of their life not being happy with what they've accomplished due to fear. **FEAR KILLS!** Always find ways to step out of your comfort zone to do what you have set out to do. (2020 should have helped with this). The thing you are most fearful that you must incorporate into your business, obligate yourself to do more of that. Whether it's networking events, public speaking, business classes, resolving past issues, or even beating procrastination. Make a plan to conquer those things with massive action, meditation, and the power of the pen. "To think is to put it in ink". Writing down your goals and writing down what you want to conqueror is like writing a wish list. It sends a signal to your brain that you are SERIOUS about what you are writing.

I read A LOT so I could recommend dozens of books but 5 must-read business and self-improvement books that I think could help any person looking to achieve success would be:

1. Think and Grow Rich - Napoleon Hill
2. E-Myth Revisited - Michael Gerber
3. The Power of Now - Eckhart Tollie
4. Profit First - Michael Michalowicz
5. Run Like Clockwork - Michael Michalowicz

Study and learn - not only yourself but the realm you are pursuing. As a society, we really have no excuse for not knowing how to do anything. We have so much content available to us. The pathway to success looks like a bunch of crazy scribbles scrambles with lots of questions like, "How did I wind up here?!". If you're following your goals and passions, you will wind up right where you are supposed to be. You ARE in the space you're in based on the moves you have made thus far.

"You Create Reality With Your Words"
- Sheena Parker

About Sheena Parker

Sheena Parker is the Founder & CEO of 4SYT Industries, a company providing Real Estate services and Facility Maintenance services to the federal and local government, as well as corporate entities. Sheena Parker has gained her experience through being a Real Estate investor, Acquisitions Manager, and Wholesaler. 4SYT Industries strive to bridge the gap between real estate and facility maintenance to government, local and corporate entities.

Sheena has served in the Army for over 18 years. As a Warrant Officer in the Information Technology Space with multiple certifications, she has excelled in both the public and private sectors as a strong female leader in the industry.

Sheena is a wife and a mother of two. She has been featured in multiple articles for her 12+ years of work as a business startup manager with her previous company. Sheena is currently a Board Member of the Veteran's Advisory Board of Dekalb County, GA. She volunteers with multiple organizations within the Atlanta area, in addition to mentoring children and adults in the areas of Finance and Business and domestic capacities. Sheena holds a Bachelor's Degree in Business Administration with a concentration in Project Management from Ashford University.

A lover of life and all things positive, Sheena loves to read, meditate, travel, and spend lots of time with family.

Find Sheena Parker online:
https://www.linkedin.com/in/sheenaparker/

"

From what we get,
we can make a living. What we give,
however, makes a life.

– Arthur Ashe

"

Empowered Entrepreneurship:
Guidance for Starting, Growing and Scaling Your Business

by Dr. Erika D. Tate

One who does not know can know from learning.
- Ghanaian proverb

Introduction

I am a learner. I absolutely love learning! As a military "brat" (my father was in the US Air Force), I attended nine schools between Kindergarten and 12th grade. It was my love for learning that enabled me to fill the gaps in my education as I moved schools and communities.

I chose to study computer engineering at Brown University because I enjoyed problem-solving and technology. Throughout my college and professional engineering career, it became clear that I was passionate about diversifying the pipeline in Science, Technology, Engineering, and Math (STEM). I spent my "free" time connecting students of color and women to tutorial services, opportunities for research with faculty, and career advancement activities.

At the University of California, Berkeley, where I completed my doctoral studies in education in mathematics, science, and technology, I discovered my second love -- community. For my dissertation, I designed and studied a blended learning experience (a combination of online and face-to-face instructional activities) that taught high school students about asthma as a social justice issue in their local community. To ensure the authenticity of this learning experience, I became a community asthma advocate.

For over 20 years, my learning and earning choices enabled me to develop skill sets and deepen my expertise across a range of disciplines and contexts. To name a few: I tested computer chips, advised engineering undergraduates, designed digital learning for students, taught community fitness classes, and recruited school teachers. Yet, my decision to become an entrepreneur was the act of love that empowered me to share all I learned with my community.

I am a social entrepreneur. With a deep personal connection to community and education, I founded Bluknowledge as a learning firm that advances equity through the design and study of learning experiences for learners of all ages and organizations at all stages.

Social entrepreneur: a person who establishes a business that solves a social problem, affects social change or makes a social impact.

Since 2012, Bluknowledge has provided me a platform to pursue social justice with some very committed and thoughtful partners. The crux of this work has been enabling equitable access to opportunities that empower individuals and communities to thrive.

These opportunities have been embedded in contexts related to workforce development, healthcare, food justice, and education. They have also focused on resources such as job training, public health insurance, healthy foods, and education technology. It is this work that has empowered me to advocate for so many communities.

About Bluknowledge

Our **customers:** Servicing organizations in education, public health, and community development

- **K-12 school and districts** seeking professional development services for their faculty and leaders
- **Research-based educators or programs** that require expertise in the design and study of impactful and relevant learning experiences
- **Community organizations and nonprofits** that contract consultants with expertise in formative research and evaluation that advances equitable, evidence-based programming and policymaking

Our core business **services:**

- **Needs Assessments:** Listen to your community. Design impactful programs.
- **Program Evaluation:** Learn from your participants. Determine your impact.
- **Research Partnerships:** Study your learning design. Share findings with colleagues.
- **Professional Learning:** Deliver high-quality content. Build a learning community.

Our **value proposition:** Creative methods. Empowering Insights. Connected Learning.

I am a mother. During my entrepreneurial journey, I became a mother -- another love! Over three years, my husband and I welcomed Katherine and Elijah into our family. Yes, you read correctly, I am the mother of two toddlers! If you are familiar with babies, new parents, or growing families, you understand that children's early years require a great amount of time, attention, and patience.

My personal decisions to take family leave after the birth of each child and decrease my working hours due to the cost of childcare had a very real impact on my business. I provided fewer services, and as a result, revenue declined. Business growth slowed.

Recently, I have ramped up and fully returned to business with a new mindset and valuable insights:

- *I have fewer women's hours to deliver services.* I need a passive income stream.
- *Children are expensive.* I need to generate more revenue.
- *My time is not my own.* I need a management and operations team.
- *Family security is the priority.* I need to access new funding that is not my savings.

My prior business experiences and changed personal circumstances are shaping my future entrepreneurial journey. I have written this chapter as a reminder that entrepreneurship is a learning experience that happens alongside our personal lives. I am a Black woman. A mother. An entrepreneur. I belong to multiple, intersecting communities with whom I am empowered to share my learning.

This chapter is intended as a practical resource, whether you are starting, growing, or scaling your business. Throughout, I share key business knowledge I have learned along the way. I provide real examples from my entrepreneurial journey and offer guidance to help move your business forward. Read. Learn. Be empowered.

START YOUR BUSINESS

In business, cash is queen! When people or businesses pay for products and services, it allows for owners to buy equipment or materials to make those products, pay people to deliver services, and write the rent check for a storefront, office, or coworking space. The more revenue (along with some strategic business planning), the more likely you are to stay in business and make an impact on your community. When you run out of money, you go out of business. Period.

My business Bluknowledge is a bootstrapped business. This means I tapped into my personal savings and some limited funds from a parent and close friend to launch my business. In the beginning, I used the profits to pay myself a paltry salary and banked the rest to maintain business during months with lower sales. As my business grew, I paid myself more money and designated profits to fund contracted team members or purchase professional services necessary to grow (e.g., a website redesign or trademark application).

The main reason I was successful at bootstrapping my business was my ability and commitment to understanding and tracking my business financials. Early in my business, I reached out to SCORE, an organization that pairs new business owners with retired executives to strengthen business ideas, planning, and strategies for growth. My business mentor, Al Torpie, offered guidance and feedback on multiple drafts of my business plan that included financial projections for 1-3 years.

Cash flow is a financial spreadsheet that details your projected cash on hand, revenue, expenses, and profits. Through my research and conversations with Al, I generated best- and worst-case projections, noting when *cash on hand* equaled zero or less (meaning you are out of business) and when monthly profits equaled zero or more (meaning you are still in business). This informed me about how much money I needed to bootstrap and grow my business.

Should you bootstrap your business?

Many in the business community consider bootstrapping a badge of pride. They commend and promote it as a measure of success. And while a sense of accomplishment is important for boosting confidence and even establishing a record of success, I would be remiss if I didn't encourage you to ask, what are you giving up if you bootstrap your business and how will it impact your life?

When you dip into your savings or incur personal debt, you put yourself and your family's security at risk. What happens when there is an emergency like a hurricane or a medical event like a heart attack? When will you break free from the shackles of student loans or put a down payment on a home?

Think long and hard about whether debt, risk, or delay is a price you are willing to pay for becoming an entrepreneur. If you choose to bootstrap your business, you better know your financials like the back of your hand and monitor them religiously. Understanding and tracking cash flow is the most important business skill I have learned and critical for anyone who plans to bootstrap their business.

Guidance for starting your business

Guidance #1: Consider bootstrapping your business IF AND ONLY IF you are in a favorable position. Use your savings or contributions from friends and family to start. Avoid incurring personal debt. Then use earned income or revenue to maintain and grow your business.

Guidance #2: Know your financials. Generate a detailed cash flow analysis that projects revenue and expenses for at least two years. Use this to determine how much startup cash you need to stay in business. Remember, when your "cash on hand" equals zero or less, you are out of business. Period. Plan accordingly.

Guidance #3: Connect with a mentor or advisor willing to share their business expertise and help you apply it to your business. They do not need to be in the same field or business as you. It is more important that they are willing to understand you and your business—customers, market, products, and services; help you navigate challenges, and celebrate your successes.

Grow YOUR BUSINESS

Now that I am the mom of toddlers and have returned to my business full time, I have been focused on increasing my sales and revenue. It's not just because there are more mouths for me to feed. It's because I have (a) less time to dedicate to service provision and business management and (b) a stronger desire for greater impact.

As I mentioned earlier, cash is queen! Funding is a resource that can help all entrepreneurs thrive. And it's not just during the startup phase. Businesses grow as more customers pay. The most common way to increase your customer base is to offer new products and services. Of course, high-profit businesses can simply reinvest earnings into new business offerings. For those businesses with smaller profit margins, owners must either save until they have enough money in their business savings, or seek outside sources, such as a bank loan or an investor. Outside funding can offer an infusion of cash that enables owners to focus their business development–hire staff, secure vendors, or boost marketing efforts and achieve a return on investment quickly–which is increased revenue growth.

After purchasing a house, self-funding a wedding, and birthing two babies within five years, it is no surprise to anyone that I would not be in a favorable position to "bootstrap" my new business growth plans. My personal circumstances required me to learn more about funding options beyond my personal and business savings. Here are the top five funding sources I have considered:

1. **Grants:** money to help businesses start or grow that you do not have to repay.
2. **Pitch competitions:** contestants (usually business owners) present their business ideas within a specified time limit to judges who determine the winners of cash prizes and services.

3. **Loans:** funds borrowed from banks or other lending sources that you must repay in a certain amount of time and with interest.

4. **Crowdfunding:** a large number of people (crowdfunders) give funds to a business in exchange for a "thank you gift" instead of equity in your company.

5. **Venture capital:** investors give you money to start or grow your business in exchange for equity - the share of ownership in your company.

To date, I have taken advantage of the first three funding categories. In addition, I have continued to provide consulting services and strategically allocate portions of revenue for new business growth.

Why should you apply for grants and enter pitch competitions?

Short answer. 1. It's free money. 2. It's a gift that keeps on giving.

Longer answer. Grant and many pitch competition monies (do read you're fine print) are usually undiluted, meaning you do not have to exchange any equity in your company for it. Sponsors of these types of funding want their winners to succeed and are likely to connect them to resources, networks, and opportunities that support their growth. Pitch competitions offer feedback you can use to refine your business planning. For any questions or advice, a judge gives you, write it down and block out time to consider it. It will only make your business better.

Example: I applied for and won a HerRise Microgrant from HerSuiteSpot. Of course, I shared the good news on social media so friends, family, and future customers and business collaborators could see I was a "winner". Later, I qualified as a finalist for the HerRise Live Pitch Competition where I pitched my new business idea to three expert judges. I won second place and additional cash money. In preparation for and during the competition, I refined my business planning and strategies, learned about new sales channels, and honed my business acumen based on questions and feedback. Now, you are reading a chapter that I had the opportunity to write because of the HerRise Microgrant. This chapter is a platform for me to share about my business, Bluknowledge; my entrepreneurial journey; and offer advice and lessons learned to current and future entrepreneurs. One application. Many opportunities.

Guidance for growing your business

Guidance #4: Consider funding options that can infuse enough cash into your business and enable you to focus your business development needs (e.g., staff, vendor, marketing). Then you can achieve your return on investment more quickly.

Guidance #5: Seek undiluted funding opportunities (no exchange of equity) that also connect you with resources, networks, and opportunities. This will enable you to grow your business acumen along with your business customers, sales, and revenue.

SCALE YOUR BUSINESS

Eight years ago, I founded Bluknowledge as a consulting services business. With a service company, you can grow your business in the following ways: add team members to carry out tasks or manage projects, focus your service menu on low-resource, high-profit activities, and attract more clients through relevant marketing channels. At the end of the day, your revenue is still limited to people hours.

To scale, that is grow your business without substantially increasing your resources (time, money, materials), you must either (a) increase efficiencies into your methodologies through routinization or automation or (b) develop a product that can be easily replicated for multiple customers with little customization.

Prior to starting my family, I established Loravore® Learning by Bluknowledge as our learning brand under which we provided service products that improved teaching and learning in schools and communities.

I planned to scale my business by developing proprietary in-person professional learning courses that could be replicated and facilitated by staff or hired consultants. The key was that once I developed a course, I could sell it to multiple customers (e.g., districts or schools) with limited modifications. Ideally, these courses would be facilitated in different places across the country at the same time.

When I returned to my business full time (in the middle of a pandemic), I decided to pivot (change business directions) and focus the Loravore® Learning brand on the development of a digital learning platform for teachers that builds professional knowledge and community. This digital solution emerged as an initial response to the ineffective training teachers received during the pandemic. Yet, it will impact future learning as teachers upskill to provide effective digital instruction and ensure that all students successfully learn anytime, anywhere.

This new venture increases the scale of Loravore® Learning by Bluknowledge. The digital format enables us to design a course once and attract as many customers as possible to purchase that course. By adding a retail page to our website, these purchases can happen anytime, anywhere. Generating revenue anytime, anywhere. Enabling me to earn money anytime, anywhere, even while I sleep.

How can you scale your consulting or other service-based business?

Your strategy for scaling will be particular to your business and market. However, I am happy to share what I have learned while planning for my service-based learning business to develop and market a digital learning product.

First, developing a product is different from delivering a service. To truly scale with a product, an entrepreneur needs to establish systems and processes for design and production and sales and marketing, from the start. Below are a few examples where mentorship and outsourcing came in handy.

Know your business financials. (I know I may sound like a broken record, but this is really important.) Planning to scale your business is essentially a new venture. New cash flow analysis will be required as well as your almost obsessive attention to its details to ensure the viability of your current and future business directions.

I was lucky and able to reconnect with my SCORE mentor, Al. Continuing our mentoring relationship has been beneficial: 1. We already have business knowledge and tools in place, such as a cash flow spreadsheet and the ability to generate reasonable fiscal projections. 2. He could clarify new business concepts, such as unit cost or fee-based vs. subscription revenue models, and suggest how to apply them in my business planning. 3. We could strategize about which funding options were key for my business vitality and long-term growth.

Establish sound business operations. As I was eagerly applying for grants and pitch competitions, I applied for and was selected to participate in the Close the Gap (CtG) global mentorship program for new ventures. Supported by Impact Hub and Adidas, CtG pairs entrepreneurs with Adidas employees to help them go from idea to market as quickly as possible. My mentor, Melanie Ovaert, a product owner in Information Technology (IT) at Adidas helped me to understand and apply the agile design process – an iterative and incremental approach to design for customers. Our goals focused on my development of a minimally viable product (MVP) with enough functionality to provide proof of concept. In working toward this goal with her guidance and feedback, I was able to lay the foundation for a design process, digital marketing content and channels, and sales funnel – the process companies lead customers through when purchasing a product (Example: Read a blog. Attend a webinar. Buy a course.)

Outsource key business activities. At this point in life and business, I am very clear about what I do best, what I want to do most, and what will make the biggest impact on my business. This requires me to outsource key business activities, such as social media, information gathering, and data organization and analysis. Recently, I hired a virtual assistant firm to support me by completing some administrative and operational tasks. This has freed more of my time to execute my role as CEO: seek funding, plan business strategies, and confer with my mentors.

Guidance for scaling your business

Guidance #6: Identify a product you can replicate without substantial resources or a service you can routinize or automate. This will enable you to scale your business, i.e., generate revenue more quickly and with less effort.

Guidance #7: Build or maintain your relationship with 1-2 business mentors or advisors. If you are in the growth or scaling phase, seek out experts to help you with particular aspects of your business finances or operations. At this point, you need less general and more specialized advice.

Guidance #8: Prioritize working on aspects of your business where you will have the greatest impact (e.g., funding or planning). Consider virtual assistants or contracted experts if you are not in a position to add employees to your business.

In Closing

Value. This term denotes importance, worth, or usefulness. The value of your product or service determines your pricing. The value proposition of your business distinguishes your product or service from competitors. This knowledge empowers business success.

Know your value. You are more than the product or service you provide. Your personal and professional experiences have enabled you to hone your expertise on a topic, process, or context. You own these experiences. They shape your perspective and inform your approach to identifying and solving problems. This is a valuable contribution to any company - yours or someone else's. Your contribution is of value. It can be monetized. It can be exchanged for cash. This realization empowers personal success.

Add value. Reflection is a pivotal process for learning. As you embark on or continue your entrepreneurial journey, reflect often. Note the following: What is working? What can work better? What do you need to work better? Share your learning. These insights empower community success.

Additional Resources

- **SCORE** - https://www.score.org/
- **HerRise Microgrant** - https://hersuitespot.com/herrise/
- **Close the Gap Program** - https://closethegap.impacthub.net/

About Dr. Erika D. Tate

Dr. Erika D. Tate founded Bluknowledge, a learning firm that advances equity through the design and study of learning experiences for learners of all ages and organizations at all stages. For nearly 20 years, she has worked to advance education and community health through research, design, and evaluation. She has applied quantitative and qualitative methods to investigate evidence-based practices that support learning and health among children, youth, and adults, individually and as families and communities.

Local community projects have aimed to increase food access in under-resourced communities; engage parents in childhood obesity prevention; and increase the number of insured children in Savannah, Georgia. Formative research and evaluation for these projects have informed the organizations' programming and policy recommendations on local and state levels.

Dr. Tate has consulted on several National Science Foundation grants to design technology-enhanced STEM learning experiences for classroom, afterschool, and community settings. She has published and presented on topics related to STEM education and blended learning, including a book chapter on Designing Science Instruction for Diverse Learners. She has designed and delivered K-16 professional development across the country, specializing in training and instructional coaching for elementary and secondary teachers that center on digital learning, STEM teaching and learning, inquiry-based instructional strategies, and project-based learning.

Dr. Tate's unique expertise and experience bridge education and public health and fosters collaboration among diverse stakeholders. She earned her ScB in Electrical Engineering from Brown University and her Ph.D. in Education in Mathematics, Science, and Technology, from the University of California, Berkeley.

Find Dr. Tate online

- Personal LinkedIn: https://www.linkedin.com/in/erika-d-tate-phd-1695211b/
- Personal Twitter: https://twitter.com/happyinmysoul
- Company LinkedIn: https://www.linkedin.com/company/bluknowledge
- Company Twitter: https://twitter.com/bluknow
- Company website: http://www.bluknowledge.com

"

"Somebody has to stand when other people are sitting. Somebody has to speak when other people are quiet."

– Bryan Stevenson

It's All About Y.O.U

by Liana Robinson

Introducing Liana

If you've made it this far in the Anthology -- arriving at my story -'Welcome!'

My name is Liana, I'm a hairstylist, Clinical Trichologist who specializes in hair and scalp, and an Afrikan holistic practitioner. Becoming an Iridologist is the evaluation of the pupil to reveal body systems weaknesses has been my greatest tool to help get to root causes. This has been my life's work, my God-given destiny to help my people look beautiful, feel better, solve hair loss problems, achieve optimum health and live well-balanced lives. And I have been walking this path from the beginning helping 1,000's people achieve integrated and lasting lifestyle changes.

I am a *'Life Stylist,'* the first of its kind, and if you're ready for a lifestyle change, call me. What is a Lifestylist? For everyone it's different. For you it could be as minor as a transformed look, a hair tip - improve your health, most importantly live a "balanced life", I hope my story will provide inspiration on saving you time with my story of family, love, and perseverance. So you can reach for the stars, and overcome any obstacles that have stood in the way of you achieving your best life ever!

Over fifty years ago, I was a shy, awkward, tall, with no hips or breasts thirteen-year-old tomboy, sporting a little afro and living in Toronto, Canada. Not at all glamorous. Growing up mulato in what I naively thought was a color-blind, tolerant, non-judgmental country, did not prepare me for racism. As a kid, I was barely aware of the fact that I was both black and white. I was just me, and in my sheltered world that was enough.

Thankfully, my family had instilled in me a strong foundation of my worth and value not only as black but also as a female. My Uncle Jerry inspired me when I entered the working world to read *Marcus Garvey, Malcolm X, and John Henrick Clarke* to better understand the issue of color. My eyes were opened and the Canadian Angela Davis (rebel for justice) emerged. In hindsight, I was to discover that the thread of racism ran through the tapestry of my life, and caused people to judge me by my color before I ever spoke a word, a sad revelation.

My dad, a proud black man, had three sets of children. Seven kids with his first wife, a black woman who subsequently passed away. Then met and married my mother Scottish Irish descent and had four more kids and two outside of marriage making me the middle child of 13. Our father ingrained in us that we were all brothers and sisters and not half- or step-siblings and we became the '*black Brady Bunch.*' He raised us to be responsible, and espoused high moral standards -- no lying, cheating, stealing -- although he wasn't always a perfect example of what he taught in his later years. The bottom line, we were prepared to lay down our lives for our family.

My dad was unique. Uncle Jerry would say, "he can step in s_ _ _ and come out smelling like roses." Blessed with the gift of gab, he could talk his way in, or out of anything. He was also an accomplished carpenter and artist, known for his carvings of women. Working with wood and glass his sculptures always featured the female form -- naked, pregnant, fat or skinny, but always magnificent.

My grandfather raised my mom, from the time she was seven, when her mom died, my mother's mothering skills hadn't been well developed and as her first child. Lucky for my siblings, she got pro- gressively better as each one arrived and became the best mom ever.

Growing up she didn't quite know what to do with the dry, curly hair. When the matted knots got so bad, she would take me to her white girlfriend's salon to have them cut out and the resulting little afro. One day I happened to see my childhood friend's mom doing her hair in two ponytails.

Although she cried through the entire detangling process, I knew at that moment that I wanted my hair done like that. The days of my boyish afro were coming to an end. Little rebellious, I started to let my hair grow.

In high school, I met my lifelong, best friend Yvette. She was Jamaican born, raised in London, and took pity on the abysmal condition of my tresses. One afternoon, she took 12-hours to comb out my matted hair and braid it. And then I hated it! The tight braids hurt my scalp so bad, after two days, I took every last braid out. She was "pissed", insisted I get another style braid this time, I happily sported my cornrows. Feeling great about my new look, I officially became a 'black girl!'

Another powerful figure in my early life was my grandfather Findlay. He wanted to ensure I was prepared for the world ahead. Just as I had a strong black presence, my Scottish grandfather saw to it that I also knew my white heritage and family. Findlay opened up my first bank account and taught me about financial responsibility. It was always me and him and our time was so very special. We spent a lot of time at Uncle Frank and Aunt Lou's house, Findlay's brother, my favorite place to go. My greatest memory of him is when he always introduced me with these loving, affirming words, "this is my granddaughter, isn't she beautiful." Even though I might have looked boyish.

Awakening

The years of my young life rolled along and my innate love of clothes, hair, world-travel and all things fabulous began to emerge. I was a caterpillar coming out of my cocoon, and my intuitive dad enrolled me in modeling school to help develop confidence, poise, and my dormant femininity. Though my priorities in high school were basketball, gymnastics, and track and field, when the opportunity came to make $25.00 per hour, I jumped at becoming a teen model and began to learn about the world of fashion.

Encouraged by my Dad, I traveled to New York every year to gain exposure to the world outside of Toronto. I used the trips to visit Big Apple's trendy stores. I soon became the 'fashionista,' of my tribe, influencing what they wore, how they did their hair, their music, theatre, and dance moves as I brought NY to Canada.

Immediately after college, it was time to spread my wings and fly out of the nest. I ended up in Los Angeles where my brother "Coochie" lived aka Thomas. Sunning, beaching, and partying became my life then love entered. His name was Skye, and with him, I began living the life of a "California Dreamer." Confident, athletic, and ambitious, Skye moved to his own beat. I adopted his bohemian, vegetarian lifestyle, live foods, and beans. We ate anything but bland and tasteless, compared to my Dad's southern cooking. So I made modifications, adding spices and familiar flavors from my youth. My friends thought I was crazy for giving up, 'real food,' and it was a challenge defending my new eating habits. Vegetarianism wasn't considered, 'cool' back then! Having battled many health issues at an earlier than normal age, including cancer cells in my uterus, bone disease, osteoporosis I might not have had the quality of life if I didn't start practicing earlier lifestyle changes of fasting, cleansing, eating raw foods, establishing emotional and spiritual peace.

Searching

Finding my dream job in Los Angeles was a challenge, I was offered a position as a salesgirl. I couldn't tell my dad that I moved to California to become a salesgirl so I continued my search. Finally, by God's grace, I landed a job at J. W. Robinson's department store as an

Assistant Manager. I was on my way. I soon met Jerry, a colleague who became my mentor. She was a beautiful black woman and a style maven. She taught me all about fashion, success, and how to live a high life in Los Angeles.

A huge opportunity presented itself when my manager had a nervous breakdown and went on leave. I took the mantle and for six months ran her 18-departments, maintaining sales and keeping employees happy. I knew I was in line for the promotion, but to my surprise, even my mentor discouraged me from believing I would get it. "They don't hire black floor managers here," was her curt explanation.

I was sure this was my niche, and I wasn't about to lose it. So I started knocking on senior management's door. Finally, they caved in and promoted me, not over the 18-departments I had managed, but to the manager of the book department. It certainly was not as exciting, but becoming a full-blown manager was a wonderful victory.

As Manager, my first events were launch parties for Gloria Swanson's and Merv Griffin's autobiographies. Gloria, a famous actress from the silent movies era in Hollywood was around 80-years old, and sported a 40-year old boyfriend; and Merv Griffin, a popular TV-personality was a delight. I was happy in this season and felt very accomplished in my little corner of the world.

Unfortunately, the feelings of success didn't last very long. More than any place I've ever lived, LA was all about your clothes, your looks, where you lived, the car you drove, who you knew, your measure of talent, and your, 'next big thing.' It began exhausting trying to find true friendship grappling with that internal conversation that asks, 'Who am I, and what in the world am I here for?' Though glamorous, this life in LA wasn't always pretty. The truth was, I missed home and began contemplating a move. New York City seemed like the next, right place -- closer to Toronto and a fashion capital -- a win, win.

Finding

In 1981, I landed a dream job at Bergdorf Goodman in Manhattan. Assistant to a Divisional Merchandise Manager was a highly visible position. There was never a dull day, as a parade of celebrities, including the likes of Barbara Streisand and Michael Kors who Dawn Mello discovered his talent.

She was Oprah back in the day…a yes from her…you were a "success".

Within three years, a completely different opportunity came out of left-field. Though it was outside of fashion, joining ABC-Sports held its own glamour and guaranteed travel. I interviewed for the job and projected confidence in a world that didn't encourage confidence from a young woman. My boss was from South Africa despite racial under-currents of apartheid he hired me to be a Program Analyst, to evaluate, and write software programs to track and manage various projects. The *buzz* among the handful of black executives was that I got the job because it was a political move, and not because I was qualified. My best friend Ingrid was from South Africa, I only knew good things about Capetown.

We women must master balance and unlike men, not let the male-dominated business change our persona. As a teen athlete, I always had a winner's side, but I'm also very laid back and mostly calm. At ABC-Sports I felt I had to prove myself daily. I developed a thick skin and my vocabulary of swear words rose exponentially to keep up with the boys. In many regards, I was fearless, at least on the outside. All I knew to do was show up every day. As I mastered my responsibilities, I became driven to achieve, and almost turned into a tyrant.

The benefits were endless free tickets to theatre, sports events. My main office was down the hall from the legendary sportscaster, Howard Cosell. We would meet strolling the halls, him with a cigar not far from his lips. My other office was uptown where all the action took place. I traveled the world -- especially exciting was the 1984 Winter Olympics in Sarajevo.

I believed I had made it and was on my way to limitless success. The technology was in, and I was at the cutting edge. Life was sweet. I purchased my first apartment and bought a Porsche and only held onto it for seven months because my aunt, uncle, and boyfriend said it was a "foolish" purchase for living in New York. I ended up trading it in for a new Nissan fully loaded.

One day, I was getting my hair done, and I observed that my stylist, a talented hair technician, seemed ill-equipped to successfully run a business. I immediately began designing a computer program that could help salon owners track their sales, manage client retention and be tax-ready at year-end. In my imagination it was a no-brainer, I was going to write a software package that could be sold to every salon in the country -- and maybe even the world -- and become a millionaire in a couple of years!

With a prototype of the program done, I went from salon to salon hawking the concept to the owners. Resistance came mostly because they didn't have the time, interest, or commitment to learning and maintaining an automated operation, no matter how I promised it would make their lives easier and their businesses profitable.

For me, coming from high-end fashion retailers and corporate America, and stepping into what was disparagingly known as the "*Betty Beauty Shop*," was a paradigm shift into an absolutely unfamiliar world. The deeper in I got, the more I saw that the salon business wasn't as simple as a bunch of blonde Betty's hanging out, gossiping, and doing hair. The challenges and roadblocks of a new industry can be discouraging, but don't let it get you down if it's your passion. Instead, be determined to find a way to get to the other side. That might mean going around it, over, or just plain through it.

I decided to go to beauty school, get my license and fully decipher the complexities of the hair industry. A small investment for the money I was going to make. Besides, beauty and fashion were in my blood and I believed I could merge the two sets of professional experiences. I registered at Wilfred Academy, a beauty school in New York while working my full-time job at ABC.

With my technology skills, I soon landed a Program Analyst job at Estee Lauder. They were in the stone ages with technology so I wrote a program to manage their newly launched products and continued to work as a consultant part-time. After graduating from Wilfred, I started my hair care career at Glemby's International. They were the only company I knew that ran their business on a computer, and I wanted to learn everything I could about that.

There's an old saying, "We make plans, and God laughs." God had an entirely different plan for me.

Clarity

It was time for another leap of faith, my prayer partner Denise and I, both made a difficult decision. I leaned on her when I needed to tap into my spirituality. She left her practice as a doctor to seminary and I was leaving the corporate world for beauty. We both felt a calling and called ourselves "The God Squad". So I dropped computing and jumped 110% into the hair business. The money came to a screeching halt and I was overwhelmed with the expenses of, "Big Apple," living. The beauty industry can be very tricky to navigate before you "make it".

As I worked to make my mark in the industry, I needed a job to make ends meet. After dealing with the loss of my sister Vickey the perfect job opened up to me. Sebastian, the top company for hair products hired me to educate and sell their products to salons. With a Sebastian business card, the world of high-end salons began to open to me. I got to work with the masters of the hair industry. Under John Atchison, who trained Vidal Sassoon, I gained my hair cutting chops, learning that cutting is all about geometry -- working with angles.

A chance meeting with James Harris at a party in Paris made a huge impact on my career. He was doing avant-garde hair for the fashion houses. I considered him my *'godfather of hair.'* Under his tutelage I learned that 'hair is a fashion and you need to know how to dress it.' I became part of his, "Hair Fashion Group," traveling the U.S. doing staged demonstrations of hair fashion trends at the International hair shows.

The transition from fashion to computing and full-circle to hair and beauty took nearly a decade. I loved the fashion, the people, the traveling, and this new teaching component. The more I got into it, the more I developed a love for the science of hair and the products being sold, I especially enjoyed teaching people what I was learning. I landed a job, for a time, as a New York educator for Avalon, Hair Care Products next, and continued to expand my knowledge of hair.

Christopher, one of my best friends from my time at Sebastian and one of their top educators was heading to Greece to freelance and invited me to join him. At that time it was the place to be for high fashion work and to perfect your portfolio. I couldn't resist the invite to do hair with him and work with the top modeling agencies, photographers, and make-up artists.

I loved Europe's less frenzied pace, and how everything shut down for the traditional afternoon nap. We worked hard, but also made time to enjoy the land and culture, and of course to party. I felt balance returning to my life. The aesthetics or artistic look of the times wanted to see black girls as exotic. High fashion print and runway shoot cast these models with big hair, leopard outfits, African savage motifs crawling out of the brush, wearing war paint. To me it was demeaning, and it made me sad.

So during each shoot that I was involved with, I would beg for a beauty shot before we went with the Dark Continent look. I wasn't always successful, but I had to make the effort. After all, God was bubbling something up in me, and it had to do with helping black women recognize, accentuate, and love their own unique beauty.

When my season in Greece came to an end, I returned to New York, where I met Lawson, an up-and-coming stylist taking Queens by storm. I worked with him for a while and even started a romance with him. Unfortunately, getting involved with the boss is never a good thing, and before long, it was time to move on again with another life lesson learned.

I landed at Adores Salon where I was on my own, renting a booth for the first time in my career. At this point my software idea faded away, I had missed the window of opportunity, as established companies beat me to market. The dream of selling my salon software package was officially dead.

I loved my new life and thinking about spending hours on a computer was not in the plan any longer.

Salon work is fun. I met Rachel, another stylist and now a longtime friend. It was instant chemistry over our love for fashion and hair, and there was healthy competitiveness that pushed us both towards growth, and our best work. It was the '90's,' and Halle Berry, at the height of her career, was sporting the best haircut of the decade. Stylists were cleaning up, making everyone look like Halle.

Rachel was the Halle Berry short hair cut ambassador," with people flocking to the salon to sit in her chair. Daily, I reasoned with her NOT to do the "Halle," on every client. It was just WRONG, to give everyone the same look, especially if that look didn't compliment her face, or her hair was in such bad condition it couldn't sustain the look. Undeterred, Rachel who was on a mission for her own salon Queens would respond, "girrrrrl, I'm just giving them what they want."

Again, there was that voice in the back of my mind, "I created everyone with their own beautiful look. And they deserve to discover, learn to accentuate, and love their own uniqueness!" If anyone's ever heard from God, you know He doesn't always give you the whole picture. And I'm pretty sure He didn't say it exactly the way I've written it, but you get the idea. From that moment, I knew I was destined to teach my clients how to discover, enhance, their own individuality and beauty.

Success

The "aha moment," of knowing that through all the years and experiences, God had been grooming me to help people find their uniqueness, was the genesis of what would become my, "Y.O.U," brand -- short for, "Your Own Uniqueness."

But let's not move forward too fast, otherwise one could get the impression that I went from a life-awakening revelation to a full-blown business success overnight. And that would be the farthest thing from the truth. Building a thriving business is not easy, especially when you're not raised in families with generational business success, and you don't have the necessary seed money to get things off the ground.

So what do you do? You go to school, you work your job, you hustle your business all at the same time until you feel you can't go on, and then you do it some more. Eventually, with perseverance and tenacity, things start to come together and one day you wake up and realize you've made it!

The success season of my evolution kicked off in 1993 when I opened the first, Y.O.U "Your Own Uniqueness," Salon in Queens, NY. Within 4 years the business outgrew that space and I opened a second salon. I was on top, at least in my own mind, and as an entrepreneur, that's all that really matters. Does it always seem that when things are going great, all of a sudden, the proverbial sh!t hits the fan? My personal life was unraveling.

My mom was trying to separate from my father but he didn't want to accept the realities of my mother's life after 30 years together.

One after another of my younger siblings took turns crashing at my house for extended periods of time because of their own personal challenges. I found love, or what I thought was love, and got married. I didn't know I was stepping into hell. He wasn't who I thought he was and none of the promises he made me ever came true. He was verbally abusive and was proud of himself that it wasn't physical. For me it was all the same, abuse is abuse.

After six years of marriage, divorce became the solution, and it was ugly, and I was depressed. I lost myself and eventually became homeless when he refused to move out, I had to get out. I lived with my sister, and girlfriend and sometimes at the salon, showering at my gym.

As odd as it may seem, this began to be one of the best seasons of my life. At this stage in my life, speaking to you as an elder, let me tell you I've gained so much wisdom from my experience. Let me encourage you to always look for the lesson in all your seasons, especially your dark ones. As it took me two years to pay back people who financed my divorce and start saving money, I gambled and took every cent I had and purchased property.

I invested in multiple properties, which became the source of income for me as I faced more challenges in life. I broke my wrist in 2017 and couldn't work, selling one of my properties helped me keep my business, employees employed and live comfortably.

The nugget I got from this struggle was a deep, new understanding of people especially women. I now have compassion that forbids me from thinking, "why doesn't she just get over it?" or from saying the Christina cliché, "I'll pray for you" but really not understanding the gravity at which they struggle. I learned you have to "stay ready" so you don't have to "get ready".

So as usual, 'good,' comes out of 'tragedy.' And as I progressed through my divorce recovery, I learned empathy and an appreciation that healing occurs '*from the inside, out.*' Also that we're going to process it individually and in our own time. This helped me as a human being and as a healer.

As I continue to free my mind, rooted in Christianity, I have taken what rings true from healing methodologies and philosophies dating back thousands of years to bring balance to other people's lives. I've gotten some push-back in earlier years that I was practicing "voodoo" but I'm so secure in myself and my relationship with God, who is my employer.

Moving the second salon in the "hood" which I felt would be a re-gentrified move. I was seeing so many young girls coming into my salon exhibiting poor language skills, dressed *not* for success, and with attitudes that were just plain ugly, which hurt my heart.

That ache birthed 'Beauty of the Heart,' an after-school program that taught etiquette through a self-esteem-building program. It grew into a not-for-profit empowering young woman damaged by father-lessness, broken families, poverty, and unattainable media images, to see themselves as beautiful, and to grow in mind, body, and spirit.

Over time we partnered with the community, and other nonprofits to broaden the scope by including teen boys and exposing these urban youth to the world. We traveled to London, Belgium, and Amsterdam exposing them to life and culture beyond Queens and experiencing everything from camping to fine dining. This ignited being a part of New York's Youth Ministry Coalition called 2020 Vision where we were at the forefront for Billy Graham's crusades Wow; we didn't see this as our plan for 2020.

Next

I do what I do today - more study, more growing, more giving, more healing - because I must. "To whom much is given, much is required," Luke 12:48. Presently under the Y.O.U, the corporate umbrella is the Queens and Manhattan hair and wellness salons, a line of hair and beauty products, two wellness books, as well as my world-wide speaking, seminars, and training programs.

Since COVID-19 my wellness business has expanded significantly - people who knew me are seeing me and referrals. Even more unimaginable is that I've accomplished all this without social media, but rather an old-school word of mouth. Needless to say, it's time for a modern business reboot. So in this season we're building websites and implementing all sorts of technological integration to streamline processes and increase profitability. It's full circle my technology schooling has come in handy as I bring my business to paperless.

My younger clients always considered me 'avant-garde-eccentric,' but during COVID19 they have sought me out. I think my light is opening them up to exploring their individuality while making life choices to look and feel better.

My, 'Go to Bag,' is always full of essential oils, vitamins, herbs, and at-home healing protocols, and I'm ready to book a flight anywhere. I'm privileged to be equipped to help people who are in pain. I'm working on relaunching *"Beauty of the Heart."* virtually. And the rest will be written in history.

There are three things I know for sure right now: *Helping people be healthy and being the best version of themselves is what I was born to do… I'm doing what I was created for…And I'm loving my life!"*

In closing my friends, my prayer for Y.O.U is to be brave, be aware, be smart and decisive, be a person of integrity, be kind, and always learn to be better at loving. That is the first "commandment" you are God's gift to mankind, *SHINE!*

Peace and Blessings,

Liana

About Liana Robinson

Liana has spent more than 40 years empowering people to find inner balance and growth. As a Clinical Iridologist, Holistic Practitioner, Certified Trichologist, Educator, and Editorial stylist, she is uniquely equipped to help you discover Y.O.U. Let Liana help you live your BEST life.

Find Liana online at:

https://yourownuniqueness.com/

"

Not everything that is faced can be changed, but nothing can be changed until it is faced.

– James Baldwin

Made in the USA
Las Vegas, NV
01 September 2021